All Pharma Research

Please return to

Head Office

The Grid® for
Sales Excellence

OTHER BOOKS by Robert R. Blake and Jane Srygley Mouton

Corporate Excellence Diagnosis, Austin, Tex.: Scientific Methods, 1968.

Corporate Excellence Through Grid Organization Development, Houston: Gulf, 1968.

How to Build a Dynamic Corporation (In press, to be published by Addison-Wesley, Reading, Mass.)

Corporate Darwinism (with Warren E. Avis), Houston: Gulf, 1966.

The Managerial Grid, Houston: Gulf, 1964.

Managing Intergroup Conflict in Industry (With Herbert A. Shepard), Houston: Gulf, 1964.

Group Dynamics: Key to Decision Making, Houston: Gulf, 1961.

The Grid ® for Sales Excellence

BENCHMARKS FOR EFFECTIVE SALESMANSHIP

ROBERT R. BLAKE
JANE SRYGLEY MOUTON

Scientific Methods, Inc., Austin, Texas

McGRAW-HILL BOOK COMPANY   *New York   St. Louis
San Francisco   Düsseldorf   Johannesburg   Kuala Lumpur
London   Mexico   Montreal   New Delhi   Panama
Rio de Janeiro   Singapore   Sydney   Toronto*

THE GRID® FOR SALES EXCELLENCE

Preface

THIS BOOK is for people who sell. A corporate president, the vice-president of marketing, professionals from R&D, or technical service groups—all may be salesmen. Those who travel a territory or concentrate on a particular industry or sell house-to-house or at a fixed location, such as a department store, certainly are salesmen.

Who is selling? and What is being offered? combine into a bewildering variety of situations. Yet underlying concepts and skills essential for effective selling are fundamental, even though applications of them may vary from situation to situation. This book emphasizes the salesman. But selling is a two-way street. Therefore, attention is placed on the customer and how to understand him as well.

The treatment is a behavioral science analysis of fundamentals of selling. It concentrates on the human relationship between salesman and customer. The approach is comparative. It examines sales behavior which is likely to be weak and ineffective and identifies underlying reasons. These are compared with approaches to selling which are more likely to be strong and effective.

Although this is not its direct purpose, Grid framework depicted in this book has been found to be of comparable interest to those on the purchasing side—purchasing agents, wholesalers, retail store proprietors, merchandise buyers, and others for whom purchasing is an occupation. Housewives, who make purchasing decisions for home and family almost daily, have found it useful as a basis for appraising their reactions to salesmen. From the customer's point of view, a greater understanding of the features of salesmanship—of what is sound and what may be unsound in a salesman's approach—can aid him or her in making more effective decisions on what to buy, from whom, when, how many, and for how much.

Reginald C. Tillam has contributed to the concepts and writing of the book. Daniel T. Davis, R. Anthony Pearson, and many other members of Scientific Methods, Inc., have offered valued suggestions. The same is true of Dr. Frederick D. Sturdivant, Associate Professor of Marketing, The University of Texas at Austin. The research and analysis on the Sales Grid which culminates in this book was begun in 1962 when the first instrument for self-examination of sales effectiveness was used. The many individuals who brought a rich and varied background of sales and purchasing experience to the study and critique of the book are acknowledged with appreciation.

Robert R. Blake
Jane Srygley Mouton

Austin, Texas

Contents

vii

facades, cloaking true intentions, building and maintaining a reputation; motivating and controlling customers, praise, concern for customers, a 1,9 facade, a 9,9 facade, criticism, initiative and perseverance; why do some salesmen employ facades?, disregard of social ethics; attainment of goals beyond one's capability, self-deception concerning one's own motivation; summary.

The Grid® for Sales Excellence

chapter one

The Sales Grid

THE OBJECTIVE of this book is to help you strengthen your selling. The focus is on you and your relationships with your customer. Try to adopt an introspective attitude of self-analysis while you read it. Look inside yourself. You will find facts, opinions, attitudes, and emotions that either get in your way or add strength to your sales effectiveness. Prepare yourself to look inside your customer by seeking his points of view. You will find facts, opinions, attitudes, and emotions. If you ignore them, you are probably building barriers to a successful closing, almost from the moment you introduce yourself. If you become aware of them and deal with them as realities, you will find yourself able to turn indifference into enthusiasm and resistance into respect for you.

The relationships between a salesman and his customer are evaluated here from a behavioral science point of view. "You-and-each-customer," interacting together, is the situation emphasized in this book. A salesman's thinking and action—and a customer's—can be analyzed separately. But in real life they occur together and so should

1

be considered in this way.[1]* The theories introduced can help you understand your own selling strategy and the reactions of customers to you. Theory is valuable. It aids you in seeing the assumptions on which your behavior is based and provides a framework for predicting the consequences of your actions. It opens up alternatives and options that otherwise might not occur to you. It helps you plan the most constructive ways of dealing with kinds of situations that may have baffled you in the past. Nothing is so practical in selling as good theory to guide action.

The Sales Grid is a set of theories about the relationships between salesmen and customers. How the theories apply is demonstrated by examining fundamentals of selling. These include prospecting, opening, the sales presentation, reacting to questions, interruptions, objections and complaints, closing, followup, and maintaining and strengthening established accounts. Communication dynamics are investigated. These encompass skills of listening, of getting the customer's involvement and active participation in the purchasing decision, and of dealing with emotions—the customer's and yours—that come into the sales interaction. This is not a book of mechanical techniques. It contains no gimmicks. It presents no pat formulas. It is not a magic pill or a shot in the arm. It is a foundation for building fundamental sales skills.

WHAT IS THE SALES GRID?

When you're selling, at least two thoughts are in your mind. One is concern for making the sale. The other is concern for the customer. These can be represented graphically in a diagram composed of two scales. The way the two concerns mesh determines your selling strategy. What does "concern for" mean? It does not indicate "how much," such as the quantity of sales volume. The emphasis is on the degree of concern which is present in the mind of the salesman, because his actions are based on his own assumptions and so emerge from them. What is significant is *how* a salesman is concerned with

---

* Numbered references are collected in the annotated list of References at the end of this book.

making a sale and *how* he concerns himself with his customers, and how these two concerns are intertwined.

Concern for Making a Sale

The idea of concern for making a sale covers a wide range of considerations. Typical expressions are shown in number of calls made, number of hours worked, number of deliveries expedited, and so on. Furthermore, the term "sales results," as it will be used, is not restricted to the sale of a targeted number of specific articles or services. It includes much more: whatever people are trying to accomplish by way of selling activities. Locating a number of new prospects is a sales result in this sense. Finding uses for a product that were not previously realized is another.

Not all selling is a profit-seeking, private enterprise activity. Voluntary associations, educational institutions, and other nonprofit organizations have ideas and programs to sell to the community and to legislatures and government agencies. Agency officials and field workers, in turn, often are trying to interest, inform, and persuade citizens, rather than enforcing laws and regulations.

Thus, "concern for" does not indicate the salesman's actual results but the character of his thoughts and feelings about how to achieve them. If your concern for sales results is low, you are less likely to take the kind of action that leads to a high sales volume than you would if your concern were high. There may be similar degrees of concern for different reasons. Company ethics and traditions, policies, practices, and training methods may be influential in varying degrees. One salesman may have a high degree of concern for making a sale because he wants his company to be profitable. Another may have a high degree of concern solely because of his desire to achieve a high commission. In both cases, the man's high concern for sales production greatly influences his behavior.

Concern for Customers

Concern for customers is revealed in various ways. One salesman expresses his concern by providing special services or a "deal" in favor of the customer. Another does so by calling frequently and chatting in a friendly fashion about trade matters or social events. A third shows concern by making an effort to present product facts and by genuinely trying to understand his customer's actual requirements. There are a host of other ways. But what is significant for the selling process is how the salesman, in behavior as well as words, expresses his concern for his customers. Each man's degrees of concern—for making the sale and for the customer—relate back to the basic assumptions he holds.

Concern for making a sale and concern for the customer are expressed in vastly different ways, depending upon the specific manner in which the two concerns mesh. The qualities of what would otherwise be identical degrees of one of the concerns will be different, insofar as the combinations with the other concern are different. That is, the high concern for making a sale which joins with a *low* concern for

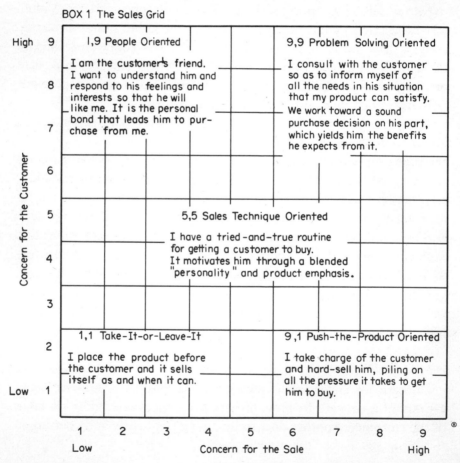

BOX 1 The Sales Grid

1,9 People Oriented
I am the customer's friend. I want to understand him and respond to his feelings and interests so that he will like me. It is the personal bond that leads him to purchase from me.

9,9 Problem Solving Oriented
I consult with the customer so as to inform myself of all the needs in his situation that my product can satisfy. We work toward a sound purchase decision on his part, which yields him the benefits he expects from it.

5,5 Sales Technique Oriented
I have a tried-and-true routine for getting a customer to buy. It motivates him through a blended "personality" and product emphasis.

1,1 Take-It-or-Leave-It
I place the product before the customer and it sells itself as and when it can.

9,1 Push-the-Product Oriented
I take charge of the customer and hard-sell him, piling on all the pressure it takes to get him to buy.

Concern for the Customer (vertical axis): High 9, 8, 7, 6, 5, 4, 3, 2, Low 1

Concern for the Sale (horizontal axis): 1 Low, 2, 3, 4, 5, 6, 7, 8, 9 High the customer is significantly different from the kind of high selling concern that joins with a *high* concern for the customer. In the selling context, the salesman's concern for making a sale and the way in which it is linked with his concern for the customer are at the foundation of his selling strategy.

PURE GRID STRATEGIES

The "Grid strategy" diagram of Box 1 shows these two concerns and the ways they interact.[2] The horizontal axis indicates concern for making a sale while the vertical axis indicates concern for the customer. Each is expressed as a nine-point scale. The number 1 represents minimum concern, while 9 represents maximum concern, and 5 represents an intermediate degree. The other numbers, 2 through 4 and 6 through 8, are placed there to denote an uninterrupted sequence of degrees of concern. They are not meant to indicate anything measurable as the gauge on the dashboard of your automobile indicates number of gallons of gasoline in the tank. But they do signify recognizable extremes—rather like "Empty" and "Full" at either end of the gauge—and also some successive degrees between them. The halfway mark is the easiest to distinguish.

In the lower right corner is 9,1. Here, high concern for making a sale is coupled with little or no concern for the customer. Prospects or customers are seen as blobs, or things to be processed in a juice-extracting way. Squeeze the oranges one by one for as much juice as you can get. Throw away the pulp. Such 9,1 assumptions can result in behavior which alienates the customer because it is so hard-driving, insensitive, and hard-sell. At one time or another almost every buyer has had an experience with a salesman who was so bent on "making his pitch"—pushing his product—that he was blind to what was on the prospect's mind; how he felt; his reactions, reservations, or doubts.

In the upper left corner is the 1,9 strategy. Here a minimum concern for making a sale is joined with a maximum concern for the customer. Under this selling style, little direct persuasive influence is brought to bear on the customer to make a purchase. The salesman is so concerned with the feelings of his customer that he spends most of his time being nice. He strives for a friendly relationship, thinking up pleasant small talk that may help make him socially acceptable to the prospect. The hoped-for sale is viewed as a by-product of friendliness rather than as a direct consequence of selling initiative. This parallels the belief that you only have to feed a clucking hen enough mash, and it will lay a fertile egg.

The desire to be likable may win friends, but this desire can be a liability to a salesman. When the desire to be liked is an overriding concern, when a salesman *depends* on his friendships for success, he finds himself in the unproductive trap so masterfully portrayed in Arthur Miller's *Death of a Salesman*. Willie Loman couldn't produce sales because his customer "friends" had retired or turned away to other suppliers who met their needs.

At the lower left corner of the Grid is the 1,1 strategy. The salesman's concern for making a sale and his concern for customers are both at a low ebb. This lack of concern for each of the basic ingredients in the selling situation results in passive behavior on the part of a salesman with the 1,1 orientation. He exerts minimal influence during the sales interview. He neither pushes to establish an improved relationship with the prospect nor tries to build acceptance for his product. His basic pattern of sales behavior is best summed up as "going through the motions." He contributes very little of himself to the development of the sales transaction. It's hard to say he's a *salesman,* but to give him the benefit of the doubt, you might call him an "order taker" or "package wrapper," even though the package he may not get to wrap up is a million dollar contract.

In the center is the 5,5 strategy, which is "middle of the road," containing an intermediate amount of both kinds of concern.

This salesman avoids a 9,1 hard push. His selling pressure is better described as sustained nudging. He shows a concern for the customer by trying to add a pleasant social taste to the proceedings. By analogy, this more resembles the synthetic smack of saccharin than the cloying sweetness of 1,9's powdered sugar. Underneath all this is a methodical, conservative attitude based on reliance on "tried-and-true" selling techniques. His pat presentation and rehearsed "sophistication" come through as mechanical.

Finally, in the upper right corner is the 9,9 strategy where high

concern for making a sale and high concern for the customer are integrated. Here the nature of customer concern changes as well as the
nature of the sales concern; the quality of both 9s here is quite different from that of each 9 within the 9,1 and 1,9 orientations. The salesman expresses his concern for the customer through such considerations as: Can our product be really useful to him? What benefits is he
likely to gain? Will he be cutting costs by using it? Does it have any
drawbacks from his point of view? The 9,9 concern is far removed from
the superficial friendliness that is characteristic of 1,9. It is a deep
concern for the customer's interests and for the satisfaction he will
receive from the product. In contrast to pushing a "bill of goods" in
the 9,1 way, the 9,9 high concern for making a sale is evident from the
salesman's thorough product knowledge which he is able to relate
convincingly to the customer's requirements as these are brought
out during the sales interview.

Other selling styles may be shown on the Grid. In a nine-point
system, eighty-one different combinations of these two concerns
could be represented. But the focus here will first be on analyzing the
corner and midpoint Grid positions and the theories and strategies of
selling behavior that they represent. In later chapters, sales fundamentals such as prospecting, opening, the sales presentations, closing,
and so on, will be analyzed for each of the basic Sales Grid orientations. These five positions are most easily understood. Later, more
complex aspects will be examined.[3]

How Assumptions Guide Behavior

Each of the five salesman theories is based on a different set of
assumptions. Each points to a fundamentally different way of orient-
ing oneself to the job of selling. *Assumptions*—things you take for
granted as being true or reliable in producing an effect—are at the
center of your customary selling strategy. If you interacted with a
customer without making assumptions about what was going to produce a sales result, you would have no sales strategy at all. Your behavior would be random, purposeless. Even so, it is not enough just to
have a set of assumptions—any old set—with a strategy that is naturally based upon them. Faulty assumptions can lead to an ineffective

strategy. People do not often ask themselves what their basic assumptions are. But it would be good for you to do so as a way of checking on your selling "health."

If you can identify your most natural set of assumptions, you will then be ready to compare it with others. You know what kind of sales results you are getting. Similarly, the consequences of other sets of assumptions can be traced through to the likely sales results. Different sets of assumptions lead to a whole range of different sales results, from highly effective to very ineffective. Would you like to check the best set against your own set? After comparing the selling consequences of each set, if you wish to change some of your assumptions, this will be possible. You'll have to work at it, for a quick mental change of assumptions does not automatically produce more effective selling action. But it is possible, and you can be greatly helped by some learning methods that will be suggested later.

Significance of Grid Positions

These five salesman theories do not define *personality* characteristics. They do indicate anchor positions for one's basic assumptions, out of which particular selling attitudes and practices emerge. They are not meant to suggest that an individual salesman is a fixed, unchanging type. Yet for some people, the Grid style they have come to live by is very deeply ingrained. For a salesman, it may have become second nature—his way of interacting with prospects and customers hour by hour and day by day. Others who observe his actions over an extended period will see such stable characteristics that they are likely to think of this man's Grid style as his personality. But it is merely his customary way of behaving as he works at his selling job. There is a pattern, certainly, but it may not be the only one he adopts or could adopt. Maybe he behaves quite differently at home under another set of assumptions.

These kinds of personal characteristics are not fixed and rigid. Each adult has already learned to relate to the world and to others. His typical behavior is in accordance with the assumptions which seem valid to him in a particular situation. Probably he has never put these assumptions into words. But they are implicit in his behavior and can be identified by others or by himself if he works at it. People *can learn how to change their behavior by making use of different assumptions.*

This is why this book can be useful to you. It will provide you with opportunities for identifying the assumptions under which you operate *now.* It will help you to examine alternative assumptions and how these underpin different selling strategies. Once you notice anything you are doing which reduces your own sales effectiveness, you are progressing toward making a change in the direction of greater effectiveness. You are aware that this need exists. Once you see how much more effective you could be, were you to replace what you've habitually been doing with something different, your progress toward higher effectiveness can accelerate. Thus the emphasis throughout this book is on introspection and self-examination.

Basic forces at work in sales situations and which determine the selling strategy that a person will apply in any particular situation come from:

1. The individual himself, as described above

2. Immediate situations (i.e., pressures of time, the need to meet sales quotas, resistance by the potential buyer, effectiveness of competitors, etc.)

3. Characteristics of the organization or trade which the salesman represents, including the traditions, past practices, and other precedents in his field [4]

4. The moment-to-moment reactions of the customer he is trying to sell

Of all these influences, the one you can most readily do something about is yourself. The one next most easily affected is the customer. This is because the assumptions that he has adopted for dealing with you can also be identified through Grid analysis. The assumptions he is making may be markedly different from yours. He is present with you, but his personal situation is different. As you know, a sales interview doesn't often conform to a pure business-logic procedure. Your immediate interest is in making a sale. He is wondering whether, if he makes a purchase, it will be a sound one. His motivations and Grid assumptions encounter yours at this point.

CUSTOMER GRID

Now let's take an x-ray of the situation from the angle of the customer. He also has two concerns; one is a concern for making a purchase. This is indicated along the horizontal axis of the Customer Grid (Box 2). The vertical axis represents concern for you, the salesman. Each

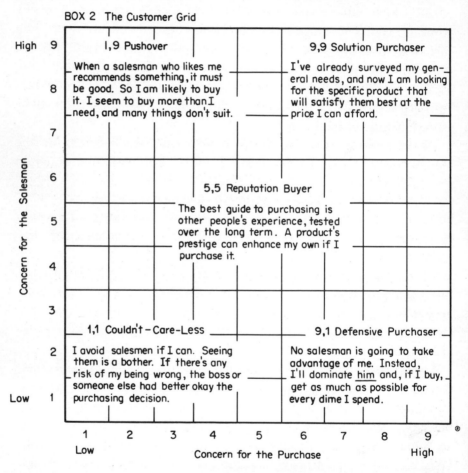

BOX 2 The Customer Grid

1,9 Pushover

When a salesman who likes me recommends something, it must be good. So I am likely to buy it. I seem to buy more than I need, and many things don't suit.

9,9 Solution Purchaser

I've already surveyed my general needs, and now I am looking for the specific product that will satisfy them best at the price I can afford.

5,5 Reputation Buyer

The best guide to purchasing is other people's experience, tested over the long term. A product's prestige can enhance my own if I purchase it.

1,1 Couldn't–Care-Less

I avoid salesmen if I can. Seeing them is a bother. If there's any risk of my being wrong, the boss or someone else had better okay the purchasing decision.

9,1 Defensive Purchaser

No salesman is going to take advantage of me. Instead, I'll dominate <u>him</u> and, if I buy, get as much as possible for every dime I spend.

Concern for the Salesman (vertical axis, High 9 to Low 1)

Concern for the Purchase (horizontal axis, Low 1 to High 9)

of these two concerns also ranges from low to high. Depending on how they combine, they reveal five basic customer Grid styles with associated assumptions, strategies, and ways of interacting with the salesman.

In the lower right corner is the 9,1-oriented customer whose maxi-

mum concern for making a purchase is coupled with minimum concern for you, the salesman. His attitude is, "This character wants to
sell me, no matter what. I've got to take control. Otherwise he'll take
advantage of me against my will." So this customer has a tendency to
turn the sales interview into a win-lose contest. Though he may purchase, it will only be after he has tried to force you to the mat. Typically, he provokes you to "prove" yourself and your product to him if
you can. Speculatively, yet in a prosecuting-attorney manner, he may
accuse the product of any number of weaknesses and limitations. He
may remark that you don't seem to know much about the product or
service you're selling. He puts the onus on you to disprove these
charges. As you complete your presentation and move toward closing
the sale, he usually resists vigorously, wrangling over the price and
pushing for extra services.

Here you are up against a closed mind and strong convictions. He
may not have a clear idea of what his precise requirements are or what
your product can do for him, but he is pushing for all he can get from
you if he decides to buy. These tendencies, if left to run riot, could
bring the result that he does not purchase although he really needs
your product. Or he may win out and take away something that he
believes is a "good buy" but which actually will not fit his requirements or give him the benefits he anticipates. You'll be blamed for
this later, of course. His high concern for making a good purchase (if
he purchases at all) is evident in the strength of his convictions. At
any particular time, he is either highly resistant to your product or all
in favor of it. There seem to be no "in-betweens" for him.

A customer acting under 1,9 assumptions is found in the upper left
Grid corner, where minimum concern for making a sound purchase
joins together with maximum concern for the salesman. He prefers to
buy from salesmen whom he likes and who like him. His desire to be
accepted makes him a pushover for flattery and compliments that
build him up as a person. He is the original patsy; a real sucker for the
salesman who shows personal interest by remembering his birthday,
his children's names, his golf scores, and his hobby interests.

What is implied by his low concern on the purchase side? There are
different possibilities according to whether he has an initial purchasing
intention or not. If he comes to you or calls you up about a purchase

he has in mind, you can assume that your competitors and their products are already ruled out of his consideration. He likes you. He knows you're handling something in this line. He's practically sold before you arrive. Unless you are conscientiously set on demonstrating and describing the product to him, there will be little more than a cursory look or feel, possibly with a remark that it seems real nice. As for the rest—quality, service, appropriateness to his requirements, and so on—all is accepted on faith. "I'll take your word for it." For him, there are more important things to talk about. If he is wandering around in a department store, or if you, as a product salesman, are making a special visit to sell him, he is easily induced to buy first one thing and then another as he enjoys the pleasure of socializing with you. Perhaps he has no real need for what he is purchasing, or perhaps he can use what he is being offered but is buying too much of it, over-committing himself or his firm financially.

When a customer possesses 1,1 assumptions with little concern either for making sound purchases or for you as a salesman, his typical attitude is, "Salesmen are always trying to sell me something I don't want. I avoid them." Usually he buys in a perfunctory, disinterested way, often not because he wants the product, but as a way of escaping the situation and the pressure it contains. It's easier than resisting. When he responds to a sales presentation because he or his organization needs something, his major motivation is to find the path of least resistance while at the same time keeping himself out of hot water with anyone else—particularly his boss—who could reprimand him for sloppy purchasing. In this situation, he must somehow avoid making any purchase that could be criticized for either volume, price, or quality. So he is likely to stall and to be a message passer, presenting the salesman's specifications verbatim to his boss or wife, as the case may be, with the minimum of evaluative comment on his part. He thus avoids attack because he has shifted the buy/no-buy decision to the shoulders of others.

In the middle of the Grid is the customer who acts out of 5,5 assumptions. In any kind of purchasing situation except the most standard or routine ones, he is tentative and uncertain. He wants to purchase something but is fearful of being taken. As soon as one product begins to appeal to him, he starts getting worried over the possibility that another might be better. He wants to be pleasant toward you, but without complying blindly with your suggestions. He is as likely to make his purchase decision based on the status of *others* who have bought as on the intrinsic quality of the product and its suitability for him. The product's reputation is important to him. He places his confidence in the tried-and-true rather than running any risks in trying out a novel product or taking advantage of other benefits.

In the upper right corner is the 9,9-oriented customer. Before the sales interview, he knows what he wants in general if not in specific terms. He responds favorably to you when you consult with him in an open, problem-solving way on how your product fits his requirements. He is prepared to be sold on the basis of facts, data, logic, and reason. He wants to know your product's strengths and limitations, so as to be in a position to close his purchase fully convinced that his decision to buy is a right one.

As is true for the Salesman Grid, so with the Customer Grid—the five positions are "pure" buying strategies. There are more combinations and mixtures than these five basic ones, taken singly, provide. But these are the fundamental sets from which the more complicated ones are built.

ANOTHER DEGREE OF COMPLEXITY

Does a salesman or customer have just one strategy or does he skip over the surface of the Grid, shifting and adapting according to how he sees the situation?

All but a very few salesmen (and customers) do have dominant styles. Each person's basic approach resembles one that is founded on either 9,1; 1,9; 5,5; 1,1; or 9,9 assumptions. But this suggests that salesmen are rigid and unchanging. We know this is not so. How can the concept of a dominant strategy be reconciled with the fact that behavior does shift and change? It can be understood in the following way. Not only does every person have a dominant style, he also has a backup strategy, and sometimes another strategy which he falls back on even beyond his second preference. His backup strategy is likely to show when a salesman runs up against difficulty in applying his primary strategy. A backup Grid strategy is the one he falls back on, particularly when he is feeling the strain of tension, frustration, or conflict. For you, as a salesman, this can happen when your best efforts meet nothing but resistance or when, at the point of closing, the customer's enthusiasm turns to stubborn reluctance.

Any Grid style can be a backup to any other. For example, even a 1,9-oriented person, when sharply challenged, might turn stubborn and go 9,1. Again, a man who normally sells in a 9,9 way may meet continued resistance from a customer. Unable to find a way of getting on to a problem-solving basis with him, he may shift to a 5,5 approach, negotiating for some kind of compromise purchase under which both the customer and himself will be partially satisfied. There are no natural links between one Grid style and another in terms of dominant-to-backup. So much depends on the individual and his situation. You may sometimes see a salesman, who habitually comes on in a 9,1 way, pressing hard for a time, then breaking off, crestfallen. He has switched to a different set of assumptions and moved back to a 1,1 state of resignation, feeling a sense of powerlessness, feeling that he is a victim of hostile fate. Who knows, had he used a different set of backup assumptions and continued interviewing the customer, he might have made a sale. It is this great variety of optional dominant-backup behavioral combinations that both the salesman and his customers can apply which make salesmanship such a fascinating profession, complex as it may seem.[5]

Apparent complexity, when you first encounter it, can be confusing. Maybe you have played with a kaleidoscope. It contains bits of glass —not many—of different shapes and colors, and these can arrange themselves in an endless variety of patterns that you see reflected from its mirrors. Children are fascinated yet bewildered by this. When the key to understanding has been found, however, what previously appeared bewildering now makes sense.

There are only ten major Sales Grid styles: five that relate to the salesman and five that apply to the customer. But the number of possible dominant-backup combinations in salesman-customer dynamics is quite large. Fortunately the linkages between salesman and customer are not too difficult to understand and use when interpreting and guiding your own behavior—while interpreting and responding to the customer's—in any sales situation. As soon as the dynamics which may formerly have been confusing begin to make sense, you are well on the way toward mastering the selling environment.

In a way, then, effectiveness in selling can be developed as an applied behavioral science. Yet it will always depend on your artistic skill in being able to sense the nuances, biases, and emotional colors in their innumerable combinations and then to deal with them creatively, moving toward a good sale-and-purchase result.

WHEN SALESMAN MEETS CUSTOMER

A step toward gaining this skill can now be taken. Let's begin to study how the Grid styles of salesmen and customers interact to yield sales results, or sometimes no results.

There are combinations of salesman strategies and customer styles that can cause trouble and result in lost sales. There are other combinations that "fit," which can result in a sound relationship that promotes effective selling with good mutual understanding and respect between salesman and customer. The question dealt with in a general way here is: Which Sales Grid styles are likely to be effective or ineffective when the salesman is facing each of the Customer Grid styles? This is done in Box 3 where the plus (+) means "likely to be effective," a zero (0) indicates "intermediate between effective and ineffective," and a minus (−) stands for "likely to be ineffective in producing sales results."

BOX 3 Effectiveness of Salesman Grid Styles

Salesman Grid Style	Customer Grid Style				
	1,1	1,9	5,5	9,1	9,9
9,9	+	+	+	+	+
9,1	0	+	+	0	0
5,5	0	+	+	−	0
1,9	−	+	0	−	0
1,1	−	−	−	−	−

These judgments can never be absolute because of the many other variable factors which influence a sale—the product itself, its price, competing products, prevailing economic conditions, the prospect's financial circumstances, the side of the bed you got up on—to say nothing of the fact that the customer's boss may have jumped down his throat ten minutes before your interview with him began. The general trends shown here are the best predictions that can be made in the light of current knowledge. The more subtle complexities of relationships between salesmen and customers will be examined in detail in later chapters.

Just one more point should be made here. There is good reason to believe that the salesman's Grid strategy is more important than the customer's. The salesman, by reason of what he does or does not do, is in a position to set the climate in the selling relationship. There is every reason to believe that the kind of climate the salesman initiates will cause the customer to respond in kind, possibly slipping quite early from his dominant style into a backup set of assumptions that are more favorable to a successful closing. Or other salesman initiatives may start the sales interview moving on a downward spiral. This is an important consideration. It means that in any sales contact the salesman *can* be a leader if he knows how. He can lead the customer to become a sound purchaser. This is what creates a lasting relationship, repeated sales, and mutual respect.

chapter two

See Yourself in the Sales Grid Mirror

BEFORE GETTING INTO the minute-by-minute activities involved in selling, let's take a quick look at you. This will help you to cut beneath the surface and to see yourself as a person.

GRID ELEMENTS

Read the five sentences below. After you have read them, consider each as a possible description of yourself. Put a 5 beside the sentence you think is most like yourself—the *actual* you, not the ideal you. Be honest with yourself.

Put a 4 beside the sentence you think is next most like yourself. Continue ranking the other sentences with 3 for the third, 2 for the fourth, and 1 for the fifth place. Thus, you will be putting the 1 beside that sentence which is *least* like yourself. There can be no ties.

These six elements describe qualities of personal behavior through which you can see your own Salesman Grid assumptions.[6] At the conclusion of the description of each element, the reasons for its being selected as basic are given.

Element 1: Decisions

_____A1.   I accept the decision of customers and others.
_____B1.   I place high value on maintaining good relations.
_____C1.   I search for workable, even though not perfect, decisions by customers and others, including myself.
_____D1.   I place high value on getting a decision that sticks.
_____E1.   I place high value on getting sound creative decisions that result in understanding and agreement.

Reaching a decision is fundamental to any action. The point where a person commits himself to one course of action or another indicates the degree of certainty that he has in making a choice. Many times you cannot turn back from a decision once it has been made. A person who can look at a situation, read the facts, and reach a decision is seen as confident in his ability to solve his problems. This confidence promotes confidence in others. A person who is wishy-washy, who reverses himself or fluctuates, increases uncertainty in others regarding his own soundness.

Element 2: Convictions

_____A2.   I go along with the opinions, attitudes, and ideas of customers and others or avoid taking sides.
_____B2.   I prefer to accept opinions, attitudes, and ideas of customers and others rather than push my own.
_____C2.   When ideas, opinions, or attitudes different from my own appear, I initiate middle-ground positions.
_____D2.   I stand up for my ideas, opinions, and attitudes, even though it sometimes results in stepping on toes.
_____E2.   I listen for and seek out ideas, opinions, and attitudes different from my own. I have clear convictions but respond to sound ideas by changing my mind.

In a world where people are expected to think for themselves, the most highly respected are those who have sound convictions that are strongly held. When a man has clear convictions, he knows what he thinks and his life has a sense of purpose, character, and direction. When a person is without convictions, or when those that he does have are easily thrown over, he is seen as weak, insecure, uncertain or anxious, or as just plain indifferent to the real issues.

Element 3: Energetic Enthusiasm

_____A3. I put out enough to get by.

_____B3. I support, encourage, and compliment others on what they want to do.

_____C3. I offer positive suggestions to keep things moving along.

_____D3. I know what I'm after and pressure others into acceptance.

_____E3. I direct my full energies into what I am doing and others respond enthusiastically.

Healthy people have the capacity for using their unbounded energy in positive and constructive ways. When they do, enthusiasm is contagious; others catch it. It produces a "Can do!" spirit of optimism and progress. When they do not have enthusiasm, life is drab and conversation is dull and boring. Then pessimism creeps in, hopelessness appears, and a sense of "Why try?" results.

Element 4: Conflict

_____A4. When conflict arises, I try to remain neutral or stay out of it.

_____B4. I try to avoid generating conflict, but when it does appear, I try to soothe feelings and to keep people together.

_____C4. When conflict arises, I try to be fair but firm and to get an equitable solution.

_____D4. When conflict arises, I try to cut it off or to win my position.

_____E4. When conflict arises, I try to identify reasons for it and to resolve underlying causes.

In a society where people have different points of view and readily express them, disagreement and conflict are inevitable. The effects of conflict can be either disruptive and destructive or creative and constructive depending upon how it is met and handled. A man who can face conflict with another and resolve it to their mutual understanding evokes respect and admiration. Inability to cope with conflict constructively and creatively leads to disrespect or oftentimes to increased hostility and antagonism. The one makes a relationship; the other breaks it.

Element 5: Temper

_____A5. By remaining neutral, I rarely get stirred up.

_____B5. Because of the disturbance tensions can produce, I react in a warm and friendly way.

_____C5. Under tension, I feel unsure which way to turn or shift to avoid further pressure.

_____D5. When things are not going right, I defend, resist, or come back with counterarguments.

_____E5. When aroused, I contain myself, though my impatience is visible.

Temper is an emotional reaction to stress, tension, and strain. Loss of temper means that reason has been abandoned and violent, negative emotions have taken over. The loss of temper also has contagious effects. Its destructive qualities can spread like wildfire. But when a man maintains a steady head and a strong hand, others have confidence that he relies on reason, and they respect his leadership. Persons who withhold their involvement and concern to keep from being stirred up also are suspect. They may even be seen as not understanding the urgency of the problem.

Element 6: Humor

_____A6. My humor is seen by others as rather pointless.

_____B6. My humor aims at maintaining friendly relations, or when strains do arise, it shifts attention away from the serious side.

_____C6. My humor is intended to be persuasive in gaining acceptance for myself or my views.

_____D6. My humor is hard-hitting.

_____E6. My humor fits the situation and gives perspective; I retain a sense of humor even under pressure.

Humor lubricates social affairs by bringing perspective into situations of strain and impasse, as well as giving richness to contradictory events. A man whose humor is sound contributes to the enjoyment of others. The person who is humorless is seen as lifeless and having no fun in him. One man brings people toward him; the other lets them walk away.

YOUR GRID STYLE

Box 4 will aid you in summarizing your rankings to answer the question, What Grid style is most typical of you? Start with the Decisions Element. Copy your ranking in row 1. Copy your rankings for the Convictions Element in row 2, and so on. Then add up the score in each column.

BOX 4 Summary of Personal Rankings

Element	Grid style				
	1,1	1,9	5,5	9,1	9,9
1 Decisions	A1 ____	B1 ____	C1 ____	D1 ____	E1 ____
2 Convictions	A2 ____	B2 ____	C2 ____	D2 ____	E2 ____
3 Energetic Enthusiasm	A3 ____	B3 ____	C3 ____	D3 ____	E3 ____
4 Conflict	A4 ____	B4 ____	C4 ____	D4 ____	E4 ____
5 Temper	A5 ____	B5 ____	C5 ____	D5 ____	E5 ____
6 Humor	A6 ____	B6 ____	C6 ____	D6 ____	E6 ____
Total	____	____	____	____	____

The highest possible score on any Grid style is 30. This means that you were completely consistent in picking the same Grid style from all six elements. The Grid style on which you have the highest score is what you see as your dominant style. The one with the next highest score is what you see as your backup. The Grid style with the lowest score represents the theory which you reject most strongly as representing you. The strongest possible rejection of a style would be a score of 6.

Remember this is a self-description. It may not represent the "true" you as seen by others. Most of us are prone to self-deception. But it is a point of departure to keep in mind as you read through the book. You may want to rerank yourself after you have a greater understanding of Grid styles.

There are two questions you might ask. One is, Are all the elements equally important in making up a man's character? The other is, Are there not other equally important elements?

The answer to the first question is No. They are not of equal importance. The *Conflict* Element appears to be the most central. When you know a person's reaction to conflict, you will find that other elements tend to fall in place around that reaction. That is why it is most important. You will see how important conflict is in the selling situation where you often must deal with objections, resistances, and complaints.

Are there other elements that make up a person's character? Yes, of course. Take for example such matters as his personal integrity and his thoroughness in pursuing knowledge, both of the product and of the customer. In later chapters, it will be seen how very important these attributes of a man's basic assumptions are. Joined with those that have already been introduced, they may be just as indispensable to the effectiveness of a salesman.

The six presented here are fundamental for clear understanding of the assumptions that salesmen make in attempting to sell. They are also foundation stones for understanding the personal characteristics of a customer. Other building blocks will be added through the book.

chapter three

Dimensions in a Selling Relationship

Now you have a general appreciation of the Grid as a framework for thinking about yourself as a salesman. The next step is to see how the Grid concepts apply to a two-person situation—the moment-to-moment interactions between a salesman and customer.

A selling relationship has many dimensions. Some are more important than others. These have been singled out for special examination in this chapter. They will be analyzed in the context of each of the major Grid styles in the five chapters that follow.

The first topic to be discussed is, What are you selling? At first glance, this might seem to be an unnecessary question. It is not. How you answer it is pivotal to how you orient your selling effort. Then the discussion turns to your preparation, including the role of product, customer, and competitor knowledge in your selling relationship. These major background topics are important in shaping the basic relationship that you are prepared to establish with any and every customer. Next, you and the customer are studied as a two-person encounter. How do you gain access to the customer's mind after you have gained access to his presence? What is the strategy of your interview? How do you close? Finally, key human dynamics in the contacts between you and the prospect are introduced. Here you will have an opportunity to examine how the customer's participation and involvement can make a significant difference in his readiness to purchase. Other issues are how your way of dealing with his objections can move him toward or away from a buy decision, and how the character of your integrity has an impact upon him and his readiness to buy. Later in each chapter, strengthening established accounts, dealing with complaints, and responding to rush business are dealt with. Finally, locating prospects, selling profitably, keeping control over your company expenses, and other matters will be dealt with in terms of the Grid assumptions which salesmen hold.

At the outset, it is taken for granted that the person you contact is the one who will make the decision to buy. Who is my customer? is a vital issue in any salesman's contact, of course. If the person to whom you present your product is a message carrier to someone else, then your opportunity to influence the actual purchaser in a direct face-to-face way may be lost. Your message can be distorted when it is filtered through another person, or you may be stalled on a dead-end street with no hope of going any further. "I'll tell my boss" or "It's up to my wife" is a reaction that the thoughtful salesman need not hear if he has answered in advance the question, Who is my customer?

WHAT ARE YOU SELLING?

The fundamental question that every salesman must answer for himself is, What am I selling? The answers may seem self-evident to you, but it is not that simple. By keeping this question in perspective throughout the book, you will notice the differences between various salesmen approaches which either heighten or reduce their selling effectiveness.

There are several possible answers to this question.

One answer is that you are selling products (9,1). Your job is to get the product into the customer's hand. If he needs it, this is a bonus benefit to him. You want to move the product, regardless of what his "best of all possible worlds" requirements might be.

Another is that you are selling "yourself" (1,9). When you have done so, your product is bought too. This is personality salesmanship. It induces you to act in ways that you think will increase your charm. It tends to lead to sociability as an end in itself.

A third answer is that you are selling nothing; the product is selling itself (1,1). When its merits match the customer's needs, a sale is made. This view of yourself as a salesman leads you to be passive and unobtrusive.

The 5,5 answer is that you are selling both—some of the product and some of yourself. You attempt to present the product and yourself in an attractive light by using showmanship and conventional selling techniques.

But there is a fifth answer. You are selling *solutions* (9,9). These solutions satisfy customer needs and wants. They solve his problems; they give him genuine benefits. Aiding the customer to understand his problem is part of selling a solution. Presenting the benefits of a product in a sound and constructive manner is another part of selling a solution. Being genuinely respectful of the customer as a thinking person who is fully capable of exercising judgment and who has feelings of self-respect is another part of selling a solution. Acting toward the customer with utmost integrity is still another condition of effecting selling solutions.

As you will see, as the Grid styles unfold, the question, What are you selling? is perhaps the single most important one you must answer for yourself. Your sales strategies are defined and determined by the answer you give. To the degree that your concept of what you are selling is sound, your selling effectiveness is bound to be increased accordingly.[7]

Why not answer the question right now for yourself? Peel off the veneer and examine your fundamental attitude as you look at the customer. What are you really selling? [8]

KNOWLEDGE OF YOUR PRODUCT

A salesman is an *expert* when he is really on top of his product and the benefits customers can expect from it. He knows it inside and out. He understands the process of its construction and how it functions. He can describe the range and applicability of its uses, its quality and reliability, and the limits beyond which it is unlikely to function properly. Being an expert, he has the confidence that goes with it. This is what people mean when they say, "Knowledge is power." With such extensive product knowledge, he is in the best possible position to sell customers on the basis of facts, data, logic, and reasoning. This means that he can design a sales presentation which is powerful because it is valid. The validity of it is what transfers to the customer the confidence of the salesman's convictions. It also places the salesman in the position of maximum flexibility for responding in a constructive and problem-solving way to customer queries regarding the product. From a longer-term point of view, it contributes something else which may be of even greater importance. Because the salesman knows his product so thoroughly, there is the maximum likelihood that what the customer buys will satisfy the need for which it was purchased or will give the customer a sound solution to whatever problem it was that he wanted to solve through buying in the first place. The buyer assumes that the salesman knows more than he does about the limitations or defects of his product. When the buyer is unsatisfied or let down, he is likely to assume that the seller deliberately withheld some of the facts. This reflects upon the integrity of the salesman, as will be discussed later.

So far, it has been taken for granted that you, the salesman, are on top of your product, that you know every aspect of it. But let's drop that assumption now. You know it is not necessarily so. People vary in the thoroughness with which they prepare themselves, whether for making a management decision, for a university examination, or for going on vacation in an unexplored area.

Some might think that quality of preparation and thoroughness is related to a man's intelligence. Certainly, smart people learn more easily and grasp facts more quickly than those of lesser intelligence. But as an explanation for preparation and thoroughness, the "intelligence" answer is likely to miss the deeper point. *A man's preparation and thoroughness is more probably rooted in his attitudes toward being prepared and thorough than in his capability for understanding.* Innate personal capacities set the outer limits to what you can do, but your attitudes make it possible either to reach your fullest potential or to miss it by a wide mark.

KNOWLEDGE OF YOUR CUSTOMER

Product knowledge is indispensable, but it's not enough. For peak sales effectiveness something else, equally important, is required. It is customer knowledge. This means knowing the customer in the sense of being informed of his problems, his needs, and his values. It is unlikely that you can aid *him* to see the benefits available to him through purchasing your product if you don't know what the benefits to him would be. Understanding his business situation is part of the information you need. More than that, it means understanding how he is thinking and feeling about his situation. Some of this knowledge is available to you as a matter of preparation before you come into contact with him. Some of this knowledge can only be developed as you interrelate with him. It is for this reason that two aspects of your behavior can strongly influence the results you get. One is listening, not simply for words, not for how to dislodge an objection, but truly to understand the man and his situation. But passive listening is not enough, because the customer may not understand what his real problem is. He needs to be aided to understand, to get a better definition of his problem before he is in a position to buy. This means that you need to be skillful and probing in getting his interest and having him answer your questions in ways that can result first in your understanding his problem and then in being in a position to forward your product as a way of solving it. This is one reason why so much attention will be placed on the dynamics of participation and involvement in the relationship you create with your customer. Fundamentally, business is a customer-satisfying process, not a goods or service-producing process. Sometimes salesmen—the people in business who are closest to the customer—lose sight of this fact. How complete your storehouse of information is, and how much emphasis you place on understanding customer needs and values as the basis of selling, will give an indication of your "actual" degree of concern for customers.

KNOWLEDGE OF YOUR COMPETITORS

Preparation and thoroughness in knowing your own product and knowing your customers is certainly important, but it is not the whole story. You could be on top of your own situation, but from the standpoint of the bigger picture, you could be like an ostrich with his head stuck in the sand. Knowledge of competitors in many circumstances may be of equal significance and value. Knowledge of competitors is not limited to technical information about their products or services. It includes being well informed as to their "total marketing" and sales techniques.

Why is it so important?

In any selling situation, you are competing with others, either actually or potentially. Though you may not see him, you can rest assured that another salesman is always waiting in the wings, prepared to compete with you for any potential prospect that neither you nor he has yet landed. Furthermore, every steady account that you have already established is a prospect for him. He knows it too and he thinks about you. His established accounts are among *your* prospects.

The natural tendency for a salesman is to identify with his own product. Positive attitudes toward one's own products are likely to make competitors' products appear less attractive—as *you* see them—than they appear to a typical customer. Therefore, you are more likely to ignore them or give them short shrift. It becomes more difficult for you to see the significance of gaining and maintaining "competitor knowledge." A typical attitude is, "I know that my product is the best. Why waste time on learning about a competitor's? My success depends on how well I push my own."

It may happen that a prospect, while listening to you—and reflecting on what he knows of your competitor's product—will then and there come to realize that he should be buying from him! A reason for this is that customers naturally want to compare things as the basis for making a decision. A comparison frame puts the customer in a position to see the relative merits and demerits of each of several competing products. It gives him the possibility of making the best choice from a spectrum of alternatives. You may be in a position to assist your prospect to make such comparisons, even when, without your knowing it, he has already begun to do so. Your contribution will be to aid him to relate to the facts more objectively than he would if left under the influence of—possibly—existing prejudices.

So much for the knowledge issue for the moment. It will be picked up again in Chapters 4 to 8 when you will have a chance to gain a clearer picture of how salesmen with different Grid assumptions reveal attitudes toward preparation and knowledge. You might want to look back at your reactions to the Decisions Element in Chapter 2 for clues to your own attitudes toward knowledge.

PARTICIPATION AND INVOLVEMENT

A second major consideration is the human dynamics that go on between you and the customer. These can be viewed first in a general way against the larger backdrop of the social scene. Human affairs are never at a standstill. Significant changes are occurring today within American society and in wider areas of the world as well. Of these, one is fundamental. It is probably the most distinctive feature of the epoch in which we live. Evidence of it appears in newspaper reports every day. You may read the signs within your own family, and you certainly encounter it in your sales work.

The dynamic is that, more and more, people want a piece of the action. Generally they are not so passive, not so tolerant of being talked at and being told what's good for them, as people once tended to be. The classic "Simple Simon" is nearly extinct. His species has been replaced by new generations who in the main are far better educated and more discriminating in their approach. All of them are exposed to much more information and wider ranges of choice than they would have encountered in the past. Young people are already sharp and sophisticated, customer-wise. Most of their purchasing lifetimes are still before them. Pat, rehearsed presentations, insincerity of any kind, or attempted manipulations by a salesman turn them off. The authority of valid, factual information is acceptable. So are authentic and friendly personal relationships. But any form of personal domination is not.

Newer generations—reared by the preceding—are on the way. So it is unlikely that the present trend will be reversed. This is particularly so, as many educational, technological, and political indicators point in the same direction. We're in a new ball game, a situation which has rendered many salesmanship textbooks, training methods, and current salesman practices irrelevant, and thus obsolete.

Let us take a general instance of where customary selling precepts and practices have now gotten badly out of alignment with the customer approach of the "now" generation. And we're not using this term to refer to the younger customer exclusively. Many older customers too are more savvy nowadays than they used to be. They may not be so advanced or up-to-date in their general education, but they have access to a great deal of magazine information about product tests conducted on the customer's behalf by independent researchers. Other mass media are increasing their sophistication.

The traditional "managed" sales interview dates from an era when customers were less well informed and more patient and formally polite than they are nowadays. Typically, its segmented and phased sequence includes introductory and middle phases during which you concentrate mainly on outlining the product to your customer. This section aims to provide him with understanding of its features and functions. Hopefully, he gains insights into its potential usefulness to him. Your presentation is factual, information-packed. You expect it may be provoking favorable feelings in him as he listens to what you say, but you have no certain way of knowing. Some salesmen recommend a brief question now and then to test the state of the customer's feelings. Many others prefer not to interrupt their factual presentation at all. Details now, persuasion later. At this moment, and maybe for several more minutes, the salesman is on stage, and the customer has the role of audience. He is expected to *think about the product* while he listens and watches. In the final segment of the interview, the salesman usually moves on from his monologue into a dialogue with the customer. It is from this point onward that he begins explicitly to build up the customer's *feelings* about the product to strengthen his desire to purchase. Most salesmen give it full throttle at this stage, as they feel that now is the time when the sale will either be clinched or lost. And it is just here that the customer often turns cold. He senses the changed emphasis, the hot breath on his neck. It is so obvious and artificial. It is an insult to his intelligence.

Of course there are many variations. Some salesmen give a lot of product information, followed by relatively little selling pressure to close the transaction. Others do the opposite. There are differences in subtlety and skill in appealing to the customer's emotions when trying to bring him to a purchase decision. But all salesmen who consciously or unconsciously keep the "information" and "selling" aspects of the interview apart, and who build these into successive phases, share a common assumption—and it is a faulty one. *The weakness is in separating thinking and emotions as though they were two distinct aspects of human experience.*

Let us look at it in another way. Every thought can stimulate an emotion if the opportunity is provided. Every emotion can promote an insight too, often creating new awareness of logical links between different facts. Is there a key for bringing thought and emotion together? Can the advantages of understanding that logic provides, and the creativity and stimulus to action that emotion gives, be meshed all through the sales interview?

It can. The key to doing it is indicated by the meaning of two words, participation and involvement, taken together. "Participation" denotes engaging in an activity. "Involvement" means being drawn in and becoming interested and absorbed in what one is doing. Involvement does not necessarily follow from participation, but here is what happens when participation and involvement are linked and integrated. Active participation in the interview helps the customer to understand the product. It also stimulates his sense of involvement. The emotions growing along with his absorption in the activity influence him to continue participating. No artificial stimulus such as prompting by the salesman is needed. In turn, further participation strengthens his emotional involvement; he feels more and more positively engaged and occupied in his and the salesman's joint consideration of the product and its relatedness to his needs. This interplay between thought and emotions that is brought about by participation and involvement is what it takes to bring about a true commitment to buy. The dynamics of full participation and involvement, or the lack of it, underlie the selling process as it proceeds from opening to closing. Grid assumptions relating to participation and involvement are presented first, as they are the silent attitudes that mold the general character of the more observable phases of the sales interview.

You can get an inkling of your attitudes toward participation and involvement by reviewing how you answered the Convictions and Energetic Enthusiasm Elements in Chapter 2.

FROM OPENING TO CLOSING

Now, let's move on. To sell something, you have to sell it to somebody. That means you have to get with a prospect. You have to conduct an interview, meet objections, and bring about a successful closing.

Getting with a Prospect

Gaining access to another person's mind so that he and you can begin thinking, analyzing, and evaluating together is not a natural process that can be taken for granted. Skill in overcoming his resistances—or if not resistance, his inertia—is essential. This applies particularly in "cold canvassing." It also may be essential when you have been favorably introduced to the prospect by a third party or even when you have been directly invited by the prospect to come in and present your product. Opening up another person's mind is an initial step which is of crucial importance for effective selling.

This initial period in the personal selling process starts with eyeball contact and handshake. When successful, it ends with a positive level of interest. While the customer's attitude may have something to do with his knowledge—or lack of it—about your product, the deeper issue is whether you and he can get together long enough to allow you to get into a sales interview, or whether you get turned off or out beforehand. You may meet three different initial attitudes on the part of the prospect. One is when he indicates a positive and receptive attitude. A second is when his attitudes are neutral or express disinterest. A third is when his attitudes are negative, rejecting, or antagonistic.

What *is* most important is how you deal with a person whose attitudes are less than positive to begin with.

The problem of "warm-up" is that of creating a favorable atmosphere—of shifting the prospect's attention away from whatever it has been resting on and getting it to focus upon your reasons for being with him. Unless you gain his attention, he may remain inert, or because his attitude differs from yours, your efforts to sell him may only promote a higher degree of resistance.

The Sales Interview

Unless he already is informed or is prepared to act on faith, the customer needs to know about the product or service he is being offered before he can reach a decision. The issue is that his decision to purchase, except under the most unusual circumstances, is one over which you have no control. Even though you may influence him in various ways, you cannot force him to take your product if he does not want to buy. The function of a sales presentation is to build a customer's early opinion that his needs *may* be met by the product into a conviction that they *will* be. This defines for you a major opportunity and also a major risk. If the customer is convinced that your product will satisfy his needs, the likelihood of making the sale is increased. If not, it is reduced. Much depends on *how* you conceive and conduct a sales interview. So "the" sales interview will not be considered here as though it were a standard form, admitting of only minor variations. Instead, in each of the five Sales Grid style chapters which follow, an examination will be made of how salesmen act under different assumptions, how they introduce and then relate products and services to customers' problems and needs.

Working through Objections

If customers were all passive and receptive to your desire to make a sale or enthusiastic for what you have to offer, selling would be simple. But only under exceptional conditions are these conditions likely to be met. The job of selling is made harder because customers think and feel. It is made infinitely harder because not only do they think and feel, but their thoughts and emotions are unlikely to be identical with yours.

When two people are interacting and when each wants something from the other, neither is certain where he stands, yet both want to achieve a result. The result that each wants to achieve is not necessarily the result that each *can* achieve. The salesman wants to make a sale, the customer may or may not be after a purchase. Under this condition, it is to be expected that a customer will raise questions that are not easily answered. Whenever an objection is raised, you and the customer are in the arena of disagreement. Just beneath the surface of any disagreement is actual or potential conflict. It is a good working assumption that an objection is never limited to intellectual considerations. Rather, a feeling or an emotion tells the prospect that something is not right. Somehow, a number of factors are not in the right combination. They do not add up. They do not fit. These feelings focus in his mind as some objection to what you are saying, or to how you are saying it, or to what you are not saying. These objections may emerge as antagonism toward you or reluctance about your product, or some mixture of the two. Every spoken objection, then, needs to be analyzed by the salesman from two angles. Is the prospective customer's objection mainly rooted in insufficient understanding or in emotions? Either can block a sale. If his objection is rooted in emotions and you ignore them, pouring out technical answers, you are not tackling the real problem. If it is rooted in lack of understanding and you interpret it as an emotional reluctance, your attempts to provide encouragement only increase his doubts. More usually, objections are partly aroused by lack of understanding and supplemented by emotions of reluctance, doubt, antagonism, and resentment. When this is the situation, both aspects must be dealt with if his uncertainty or lack of interest is to be converted into positive convictions.

The manner in which you meet objections or disagreements can make the difference between a sale or the loss of one. Effective prospecting, even a sound sales presentation, may lead to nothing, depending on how you handle objections. This is so central with respect to selling that it needs to be studied deeply and well as the basis for increasing sales effectiveness. You might now want to look again at the Conflict, Temper, and Humor Elements in Chapter 2 to review where you are likely to stand on this issue.

Closing

The behavior of people sometimes undergoes dramatic change as they near the point of decision. A customer can be free, open, candid, and constructive during the sales presentation, creating the impression that he has every intention to buy. But at the point of decision he reverses his field. He may ask for time to think it over, or procrastinate in some other way. Maybe he chooses this moment to introduce objections which the salesman thought had been resolved a long time before. Alternatively, as the closing is approached, he may bypass the steps essential for a sound decision and tell you his negative decision as though his mind is already made up. Or he may act as though it was never his intention to arrive at a decision in the first place.

Behavior during that interval between just about completing the sales interview but before reaching a decision is, in other words, often difficult to explain or account for in terms of what has occurred during your discussion with the customer. Why is this?

Rehearsing a possibility in one's mind is quite different from committing one's self in a positive act of decision. The first is "as if"; the second is for real. There tends to be less anxiety or uncertainty in a person's experience of his own emotions when he is rehearsing. But often new emotions arise when he is acting for real. It is the difference between practicing a speech in private and standing before a live audience where one's actions have real consequences for one's self. Because the closing converts what was formerly an interest in buying into a positive or negative decision about doing so, it is a very important point in a salesman's relationship with his customer. The idea to be appreciated here is that new tensions which can disturb the customer's constructive thinking may enter his mind as he feels himself confronted with committing himself and his pocketbook. An analogy may help here. It is one thing to make a matrimonial pitch when the wedding day seems far ahead in the future; it is quite a different feeling when you are facing the altar, about to get involved in a binding contract. This is like the problem of closing a sale. From the customer's point of view, is the pleasure of the product greater than the pain to his pocketbook? He inevitably arrives at a buy/no-buy decision, and your job in closing is to deal effectively with these subtle tensions to bring about a positive result.

ESTABLISHED ACCOUNTS

Once the first sale is made, the question becomes, How do you turn your new customer into a steady one from whom you can enjoy increased sales volume? Once a successful closing has been reached, any initial objections that he had or resistances that you encountered have subsided. You are in accord, at least for a while. Even more important, if he remains satisfied with the product, the likelihood of his shifting from your product to a competitor's is greatly reduced. This brings you to a point of maximum opportunity, and it also confronts you with a higher-risk situation.

What are the opportunities and what are the risks?

Maintaining Accounts

One opportunity is you are in a favored position. He understands your product. If he is presently satisfied with it and with his established relationship with you, you can build upon what you have already achieved. This provides a basis for increasing your sales results. It also affords you additional time that can be put into prospecting elsewhere, since much background effort has been invested that need not be repeated.

What are the risks? The major risk lies in any mental attitude that may drift you into complacency. Since the natural tendency is to feel you "have him in the bag," your calls on him may be less frequent than would be desirable for sustaining his interest. Or, if there is competition for your time and some shortage of your product, the inclination might be to make him wait while you divert the product to a new customer. This same attitude can erode your servicing of his already completed purchases and can lead to your giving less weight to his complaints than they merit. What are the consequences for your relationship with an established account if you adopt these slovenly attitudes? His initial satisfaction can slide away, and at the extreme can turn into resentment. Before you know it he may be saying, "I'll show that s.o.b." His way of showing you is to turn to your competitors on the assumption that they will do for him what you are failing to contribute.

Complaints

The combination of a salesman who has just the right products and the one-in-a-million customer who never has a complaint is hard to come by. This ideal set of circumstances would mean that the ultimate in satisfaction had been reached. Reaching it is as unlikely today as it will be tomorrow. In the realistic world, things go wrong. The product does not do everything it was expected to do; delivery is tardy; a defect appears in the early phases of the product's use; a service call which was needed was not made on schedule. A host of these and other problems inevitably arise. If you are lucky, the customer will complain. If you are not, he'll just go silent and his business will go to your competition next time.

Dealing with complaints is different in some significant ways from handling objections during the sale itself. In handling objections successfully, you are raising the expectations of a customer that he will get what he is after—or even more than he anticipates. But complaints arise because his expectations have been violated. The source of almost every complaint is faulty products or services which fail to yield the benefits anticipated. Violated expectations which are not successfully resolved can quickly turn good feelings toward you and your products into antipathy or wrath at your indolence. Objections most frequently are based on thinking and reason, lack of information, or faulty logic. The reaction that accompanies almost every complaint is drawn from the reservoir of emotions. These are not the emotions of warmth or enthusiasm. Rather they are the emotions of disappointment or possibly antagonism from the feeling of having been hoodwinked or sold a bill of goods, or being a victim of an unfulfilled promise.

How complaints and the emotions beneath them are dealt with may very well determine whether an established account can be retained and strengthened or whether it will be blown to smithereens. A kind of basic human attitude can get in your way unless you recognize it and avoid letting it adversely influence your behavior. The basic tendency is to turn away from the unpleasant, not allowing your own feelings to be stirred up. You are fearful of any risk of getting into a fight with the customer on whom you are dependent for your success. Negative emotions are catching, and when a customer complains, it is easy for you to catch his disease. Not that you respond with complaints about him. Negativism on your part emerges as you procrastinate and try to wiggle your way around rather than facing up to the complaint and taking the actions essential for reducing his frustration.

Rush Business and Special Requests

If it is possible to program the product requirements of established accounts without straining the company's production capacity and if all current customer needs can be satisfied through optimal factory scheduling and production, one of the deeper problems of servicing established accounts will have been eliminated. As long as there are still openings in the upcoming production program, you will have little trouble coping with fresh business. But this happy state seldom lasts. It is inevitable that customer orders for products will not jibe perfectly with factory production cycles. Under these circumstances you, the salesman, are really the man in the middle. You come under pressure from the customer to get his order through in a hurry, with his pressure sometimes implying that you are a superman who can respond instantaneously to his every request. If you fail to meet a customer's request for rush deliveries, you risk losing his future business.

Conversely, you sometimes come under pressure from your company. The factory manager might want you to get the customer either to defer or at other times to speed up the previously agreed delivery schedule. The factory aims to keep its production-warehousing-distribution flows as steady as possible. Sometimes the customer agrees readily, if this poses no inconvenience to him, but at other times he balks and holds you to the previous commitment "or else. . . ."

So it is not unusual, as a salesman, to find yourself between conflicting pressures from customer and company sources. In rush-business situations and when sudden special requests are made from whatever quarter, the pressures increase. All the important qualities of your personal behavior—the Grid elements—are called upon for dealing with them, as are those of your company colleagues and the customer. The outcomes can range from full reconciliation with problem solution, to battle scenes, unsatisfactory compromises, or a variety of escape tactics that leave various kinds of chaos in their wake. Let us search for "best outcome" strategies as the analysis continues.

INTEGRITY: CREATING VALID EXPECTATIONS

Many studies by salesmen who have observed themselves and their salesmen colleagues through their careers speak as with one voice concerning a salesman's integrity. It is certainly a major contributor to his continued success. From the outside, integrity is seen as an unfailing consistency between what a man says and what he does. Customer confidence is founded on the premise that what he is being asked to buy is what the salesman really is selling, that the needs he anticipates satisfying will be satisfied. This means that the product does what it is described as having the capacity to do. It benefits the customer in the ways that he is led to expect it will.

A salesman with integrity is one who helps the customer to have a valid set of expectations regarding how well the product will solve his problem. The distinction between what a person is actually buying and what he thinks he is buying is contained in the difference between the realistic properties of the product and his expectations of it. He can be led to have a set of expectations that it will do something, only to find out when he starts using it that it doesn't. Then his expectations are violated. He is frustrated, dissatisfied, unhappy, and feels sold down the river. If his expectations are satisfied or exceeded—that is, if the product does all or more than he had believed it would—his esteem for the salesman tends to increase. So the question of whether or not the customer's expectations are fulfilled by the product or are violated is related to how the product is presented to him and to the salesman's carefulness in detailing what it actually can or cannot do. Unrealistic customer expectations can be corrected if you check to find out what his current understandings are *before* he purchases. Here is where you either maintain or lose your reputation for personal integrity, depending on whether your customer is satisfied or frustrated by the consequences of his purchase.

SELF-MANAGEMENT

Salesmen are the most freewheeling individualists in our modern business society. A salesman is usually under supervision from some central point. But in the final analysis, he is on his own. He is his own manager.

How you manage yourself is up to you.

Managing Your Time

Time is worth nothing in itself. It's what you do with it that counts. Some say, "Time is money." Others say, "Time on my hands," and still others, "No time to think." The deeper point, of course, is that there are only so many hours in a day. How you think about those hours and what use you make of them is the all important issue. If you let time slip through your fingers so that it's gone before you know it, with nothing accomplished, you're not going to sell much. If you organize yourself to make good use of all available time, getting an effective yield from every moment at your disposal, then time *is* money—in your pocket.

The effectiveness with which time is used is a very personal matter. Often explanations are given such as, "Frank is well organized; he knows how to use his time," or "Tom jumps from one thing to another in such an erratic way he has to be held together with wire." A more probable explanation of how time is used points to the factor of your attitudes rather than to any inherent quality you might possess. Since the way you use your time is influenced by your attitudes, then if it becomes clear to you what these attitudes are, the next step is easier to take. This is to learn the skills of using your time more productively. Personal planning and scheduling are at the heart of it.

Locating New Prospects

A professional approach to selling can result in unending excitement as you explore new business opportunities. A self-evident truth is, If you can't gain access to a potential customer, you can't sell him. You may have extensive regional territories to cover. Prospects aren't as easily recognizable as features of the landscape. They have to be actively sought out. They have to be discovered before any sales approach can be made. If this is not done, they'll go unnoticed, like buried treasure. Or you may operate within a small space area, such as in a retail business. Even so, you can locate new customers "on the outside" and gain access to them.

In most sales organizations, people differ a lot in the degree of interest they have in searching out new prospects. They differ in how successful they are in finding them. Some are vigilant, eager, and quick to try out new approaches. Others, less so. One man's assumptions restrict his exploratory vision like a set of blinders. Another's fit him with perceptive radars which constantly scan for new selling opportunities.

Servicing

The narrow view of selling is, Once sold, that's it. But there is a broader view too. It is this: the organization that sells has not completed the sale until the customer is on stream with the purchase that he has made.

That period of time after the product has been delivered but before it has been brought into use can be regarded as an integral part of the sale. Many problems can arise during this period. How you handle them can add to the customer's glow or cause him to glower. You are the natural liaison man that the customer turns to in the hope of dealing with unanticipated problems in making use of the product. But you may be developing other business elsewhere. Possibly you feel that you are not making the best use of your time if you go back to the customer you've already sold. Nor, conceivably, will you be the best person to handle the situation. Yet customer demands on your time are likely to be felt here too.

Selling Expenses

Another aspect of self-management relates to your attitudes toward the expense items over which you have direct and personal control. One company's practices might be that a salesman's objective should be to keep his expenses to a minimum. In this way, maximum profit could be obtained from each selling activity. At the other extreme, expense control can be so loose that unjustifiable practices are tolerated. Sales managers know that the first-mentioned "rational" business approach is often ignored, and for understandable reasons when viewed from the standpoint of the salesman. Salesmen often bring up striking examples of how some expenses, which they incurred in the course of promoting their sales, have paid off. They tend to forget the frequency with which other promotional expenses did not. The salesman's attitude may well be, "In case of doubt it's better to load on a little expense in going after a sale than to risk losing it by not being willing to run up additional money." These are matters of judgment, subtle but significant. Usually the salesman's own freedom of judgment is narrowed by his company's expense policy and standard practices. It might be that these are so constricting that the flexibility of judgment he should have is not available to him.

Sound expense guidelines are desirable both from the company's and the salesman's viewpoint. But in the final analysis the bang per buck of expense—in terms of sales results—depends on your judgment.

Self-steering

If you maintain sound attitudes toward steering yourself, you can look forward to improving your effectiveness continuously through your sales career. Since you need to think and plan before taking further action, action which may need to be different from what you have been doing in the past, it is important to know how you are currently thinking about this matter of self-steering.

Profitable Selling

Everything up to now has been based upon a business premise. It may be justified; maybe it's not. It needs to be unveiled and looked at hard and square. The premise to be examined is basic to all business. It comes to a point of critical significance as a salesman's attitudes toward it are revealed in his selling behavior. What is selling for? In a private enterprise society, selling is for profit. It is as simple as that. But profit is not simple. The reason is that from a long-term standpoint the only sound profits come where and when customers' needs are met, and their satisfaction with your products increases steadily year by year. Profitable selling results when real earnings accrue from your sales efforts, and your products have your customers' endorsement.

The assumption which might be made is that all of the above is self-evident. It is not so. Some salesmen have reached this basis of understanding, but many haven't. Often it is thought that if a salesman concentrates on pushing his product, profit will automatically result. But, of course, products move better when they have a razor-thin margin and are decorated with expensive and oftentimes unnecessary services. Then a salesman can easily look at his sales volume, thinking he is making a contribution to the corporation when, in fact, his performance may add expense rather than profits. To counteract this, company executives are likely to formulate marketing policies which put the salesman in an inflexible straitjacket. If he can act effectively within the straitjacket, he can contribute to corporate profitability, but the inflexibility may be such as to reduce his capacity to sell.

Where a company's marketing policies are unsound or unclear, or both, sales managers and their salesmen adapt to the situation in various ways. The likely impact of various selling strategies on profitability will be examined throughout the book in the context of each Grid style.

CONCLUSIONS

There are four conclusions from this brief survey of each of the major dimensions of a salesman-customer relationship which can be checked out further as you proceed. They are:

1. Your concept of what you are selling, with the associated knowledge that you gather and apply, will largely determine the characteristic strategy you adopt for dealing with customers.

2. Your view of what is the customer's part in the interview will influence the way you open with him, how and what information is provided, your response to objections, and the way in which a closing is brought about.

3. Your personal integrity, which comes under review during and after every sale, relates importantly to whether or not you will build

up a long-term selling relationship with the customer, based on mutual respect and confidence.

4. Your attitudes toward self-management will be significant factors in determining the extent to which your selling is profitable to you and to your company.

Chapters 4 through 8 examine how the salesman-customer relationship is most likely to take shape in each of the major dimensions and as a whole, depending on whether a salesman's behavior is founded on 9,1; 1,9; 1,1; 5,5; or 9,9 assumptions. A separate chapter is devoted to each of these Salesman Grid styles.

As you read these chapters, you are likely to find something of yourself in each of them. This is natural, as the descriptions presented are "pure" styles and very few people are as consistent as that in their everyday actions. But one of them is likely to be more characteristic and therefore a better description of you than any of the others. Another one will probably be next most like you. When thinking about the Grid assumptions that are characteristic of you, remember the difference between intentions and actual behavior. Good intentions are one thing, but actual behavior determines the results you get. You can avoid self-deception to the extent that you're able to separate what you *think* from what actually occurs—how you come through to the customer. The following chapters are intended to help you to heighten your awareness of what really happens while you are selling under your current Grid style assumptions.

chapter four

9,1

THE PERSONAL BEHAVIOR of a salesman who acts on 9,1 assumptions is motivated by his drive toward mastery. He is *achievement-oriented*: he wants to prove himself through high performance. Consequently, he has an inner sense of direction, all his own. Other people's opinions, which might require a shift from his present course of action, are disregarded. He tends to be impervious to criticism. If anyone is disagreeing with him or otherwise standing in his way, there are no second thoughts about arguing him down—he does it.

Having this orientation, the salesman is highly committed to making and getting decisions and then sticking with them. He wants to do things his own way because he feels he has the right answer for others as well as for himself. So his convictions are very strong. He is ready to stand up for his own ideas, opinions, and attitudes and to press forcefully for their acceptance, even when others are pushing their own points of view against his. These strong convictions move him to initiate action, to grab the ball and run in his own direction with enough impetus to overcome the opposing forces. Though he may not always be right, he is seldom in doubt. Categorical thinking of the right-or-wrong sort is his characteristic mode. There are few if any grays. Once he takes a position or sets his course, he is likely to hold to it tenaciously. When this becomes his customary way of relating to life, the 9,1-oriented person is more inclined to interpret the facts so as to uphold his own views than to make his conclusions consistent with the objective situation.

Furthermore, this self-sealing tendency keeps him detached from the worlds of other people. He brings his general desire to "win" into the sales interview situation. His approach to the customer may be friendly, but this is conditional. He is pleasant as long as he feels himself to be the driving power moving the customer along toward a positive buying decision. If the customer bows to the salesman's will and allows himself to be influenced, all is well. The warning light comes on, though, if the customer questions what he is saying. To the salesman, this means that the interview is in danger of veering out of control. Usually his first reaction is to try to override the customer's disagreement or bury it. If the customer persists, now the time has come to show him how wrong he is. A salesman who is acting under 9,1 assumptions finds little reason to shy away from conflict. Upholding the validity of his position is more important than maintaining friendly relations with the customer. "It is weak to let yourself be challenged." Momentum builds up as he argues with the customer, and he is quite unaware of the impact his words may be having. His temper can easily become involved when things are not going according to his wishes. His humor, like his approach to conflict, is hard-hitting. It tends to carry a sting. The total effect—of which he remains unaware until it is too late—may be that his behavior goes beyond the customer's tolerance limit. Suddenly the interview is broken off, and another sale is lost.

KNOWLEDGE: PRODUCT, COMPETITOR, AND CUSTOMER

9,1 assumptions strongly influence a salesman to get to know his product up one side and down the other. He makes himself an expert, a real specialist. He wants to be sure that he will never be caught short by anyone—that would be defeat. Product knowledge is one of his strengths. His attitude is that his product is good—and good for the customer—no matter what the customer thinks.

The same basic attitude impels him to get to know who his competitors are and what *they* are pushing. He knows he is in a win-lose fight with them. If the competitor wins, he loses, and vice versa. To be done in by a competitor is a bitter pill to swallow. Because of this attitude, the salesman is likely to have probed the competitor's strategies, pricing, and product characteristics for any weakness or defect, real or reputed. This too can add strength, if he uses the facts he has to demonstrate the relative merits of his own product compared with the competitor's. When dealing with his customer, he uses this knowledge as ammunition for shooting down the competitor, maybe not by name, but the implications are clear. The likelihood of his making the hit depends partly on how well grounded his criticisms are and partly on whether or not the customer is already favorably impressed with what the competitor is offering. The salesman's strong "he's no damn good" attitude can sometimes influence the customer against the competitor's product. Their now shared antagonism against the third party can promote some feeling of solidarity between customer and salesman. However, when the customer *does* already have respect for the competitor's product, having known of it and maybe having used it himself for some time, he will not admire the salesman who knocks it. To the customer, such a salesman appears unfair, arbitrary, and unworthy of trust. The salesman has done himself in; unwittingly, he has been selling his competitor's product rather than his own.

In contrast to his well-developed product and competitor knowledge, the 9,1-oriented salesman's customer knowledge is likely to be little more than a veneer. Being so unconcerned for customers as individuals, he sees no need to prepare himself in advance or at the beginning of the interview, to understand the person's unique situation with its accompanying needs. The question, What are the unique circumstances facing this customer? is remote in his mind. To his way of thinking, a customer is a customer is a customer—all exist for the purpose of being sold. If a person volunteers information about himself, the salesman is only listening for an entry point into which he can wedge his product's benefits as the standard solution to any problems the customer has.

PARTICIPATION AND INVOLVEMENT

The 9,1 attitude influences a salesman to take over and dominate the interview. He tries to mold and shape most of the customer's responses and to suppress others. Objections to the product are out of line. He is not interested in the customer as a person who has unique thoughts and emotions and special needs of his own. He, the salesman, is going to tell him and then sell him. Listening is all important. It is the customer who is expected to listen. There will be no time wasted so long as the customer stays quiet. It does not occur to the salesman that a customer's spontaneous participation in the interview could quicken progress toward a favorable buying decision. The customer participation he wants is the agreement to buy—a nod, a brief word, or a signature—as soon as the sales talk is over.

As he sees it, to invite customer participation is to invite trouble. Thus, his use of questions is likely to be in one of two ways: a rhetorical question which permits the salesman to answer himself so as to emphasize a selling point, or ones calculated to get a customer to respond Yes in a way that commits him to purchase. He thinks customers are crafty, always looking for excuses to get out of buying something. Give them half a chance, and they'll start bringing up all sorts of objections which will then have to be overcome. The salesman is ready and willing to do this should it become necessary, but he does not want to waste time. It is better to rush the customer into a quick buying decision and then move on to the next prospect.

Of course, many customers are not so passive as the salesman wants them to be. They rebel by interrupting, talking about what *they* want. The salesman jumps in as soon as he detects an opening for counterargument. This enables him to shut the customer up while he goes on with his spiel. When he has a customer who listens quietly without commenting or interrupting, the 9,1-oriented salesman delivers his standard speech in a forceful style, sometimes going on for longer than would be necessary if he had a way of knowing when the customer was feeling ready to purchase.

In these and other ways the salesman who behaves in a 9,1 manner cuts himself off from possibilities of sound involvement with the customer. Little real back-and-forth discussion develops of the sort that could lead to a logical and emotion-reinforced decision by the customer that the product fulfills his own or his company's needs. Any of his prior misunderstandings about the product are likely to be retained. His present prejudices against the product, if any, are reinforced, and maybe new ones are created as a result of the salesman's powerfully exploitative approach.

Opening

The salesman jumps in with a hard, driving approach to get attention. He avoids taking No for an answer, even in the initial few moments. He does not allow himself to be put off, even when the prospect tries to turn him off. His goal is to keep talking, to keep the conversation alive on a never-say-die basis. He might say, "This is going to take no more than five minutes of your time. I can explain it briefly. You will immediately see its advantage."

Here is a salesman who tries to cut to the heart of the matter. No folderol, no irrelevant remarks about the weather, the painting on the wall, the rug on the floor, no casual inquiry about business conditions. Instead, he comes on at full pressure to gain an opening, to get and to keep the customer's attention. Once he has a grip on the customer's mind, he is determined not to let go. He's like the old farmer who hits his mule between the eyes to get his attention.

Sales Presentation

After gaining access to the customer's mind, the 9,1-oriented salesman assumes there is now a one-way street for him to drive along, with nothing coming the other way. He is going to sock it to this customer and make him believe. Here is where his product knowledge can score.

More than any other salesman, the 9,1 hard seller cultivates and uses an impressive appearance, voice, and manner to give weight to the content of what he is saying. He might start by listing the array of benefits to be gained through purchase of the product and then proceed through his major selling points, all of them calculated and marshalled to prove that their benefits are for everyone. His points of emphasis are the ones he has selected mainly for their dramatic possibilities. On first glance this might appear as a "customer-oriented" presentation since his emphasis is on benefits and satisfactions. In truth it is not. The reason is that there is no genuine exploration with the customer of what his situation is. Consequently, there can be little matching of needs to possibilities. Without this kind of exploration the question that is answered is, What can the *product* do? not, In your situation, this is what you can expect from our product when you use it.

This kind of sales presentation is not only a one-way street, it is also one-sided propaganda. The product's positive features are emphasized to the limit; its inner performance boundaries are ignored. Along the way, the weaknesses of competitors' products may be detailed. The general theory is that by keeping the customer's attention solely focused on the benefits and favorable aspects of his own product, standing out from the dark background of other products' defects, the customer has no option but to be persuaded of the wisdom of making the purchase.

The whole presentation is calculated as a high-pressure pitch which gives little opportunity for doubts or reservations to arise in the customer's mind. It's calculated to be highly persuasive. The evidence has been carefully selected so as to anticipate and prevent customer objections or to divert them if they arise. A customer must never be allowed to say No. The salesman has few scruples about causing the customer to overcommit himself financially. In these ways, the 9,1 sales presentation boxes the customer in and, as intended, makes it difficult for him to escape. Carried to an extreme, 9,1 is characterized by the "snake oil" salesman so often seen in motion pictures. Salesmen such as these have given the entire profession a black eye.[9]

Objections

If the customer manages to get a word in, to put forward an objection, or to lodge a criticism, how is the 9,1-oriented salesman likely to react? Objections are a sign that a contest is on. They are likely to precipitate a win-lose orientation and to intensify his categorical thinking rather than to promote a problem-solving orientation where he seeks to understand the customer's mind and emotions as the basis for working through a disagreement. It is difficult for a 9,1-oriented salesman to refrain from polarizing issues. The reason is that an objection is a challenge. And the strength of his conviction is likely to increase with a challenge, since he is likely to shield his position and protect it rather than to open up his thoughts to critical examination. If another person's attitude does not square with his thinking, it is neither examined nor evaluated; it is rejected.

The most typical response would be to overwhelm the objection. This can be done in several ways—by the piling up of "evidence" as a rational approach or by suppression tactics which ignore the emotional overtones of the customer's reaction. He might deal with the objection by giving the customer ten reasons why he is wrong and then getting him to admit it. Or he makes him look silly either by pulling the rug out from under him or through ridicule. Some hitherto unrevealed information is produced to nullify the objection. Another tactic, by no means unusual, is to ignore the objection as though it had never been spoken and to press on with his sales presentation. The salesman seems deaf to the word No. Alternatively, the salesman might simply cut off the customer's statement and suppress him by an attitude that implies, "Yours is not to question why." The consequences of these win-lose attitudes toward objections may be that while some of the prospect's intellectual misunderstandings emerge and are dealt with, other emotion-based objections persist and can be reinforced by resentment at the way in which he has been put down by the salesman.

Closing

The 9,1 doctrine is to strike while the iron is hot. At the end of his presentation the salesman pushes for a close then and there, to get the deal clinched as rapidly as possible before anxiety and doubt have had an opportunity to shape themselves in a customer's mind. He has his pen ready and maneuvers it into the customer's hand for a closing signature at the moment his spiel is completed. If the customer still hesitates, he puts on the squeeze as much as he can. "There are only a few left," "You'll be making a great mistake if you don't buy now,"

"It's an opportunity you shouldn't miss," and so on. Customers who are plagued with indecisiveness and have trouble "making up their minds" can be boosted into confidence by the salesman's strong endorsement of the product and his assurance that their decisions will be sound ones. Those who prefer to convince themselves are likely to become more resentful as the pressure increases.

ESTABLISHED CUSTOMERS

A salesman who acts on 9,1 assumptions is inclined to treasure an established account much as a dog guards its favorite bone. Once a customer is sold, he's his. The salesman is on his side now and extends him the protection and benefits at his command.

Maintaining Accounts

Because of his intense ambition to raise his sales volume, he may unwittingly concentrate his emphasis on the larger accounts and not make much additional effort to cultivate the marginal or low volume accounts. But whenever he loses an account, however small, he is a tiger trying to get it back. He is likely to feel that the customer has treated him unfairly. He fails to recognize that he has been neglecting those actions that would have helped to nurture many of the small, uncertain accounts into steady ones. With regard to more lucrative accounts or those that have potential for increased volume, no amount of effort is too much if this is what it takes to retain them.

Complaints

Complaints from customers quickly activate this salesman. He is in danger of losing his preeminence. So he speedily gets alongside the customer and does whatever he can to bring him around. His aim is to keep the problem in bounds and prevent it from looking as bad as it might be or worse than it can become. Just as during the sales presentation, he tries to dominate the discussion, but this time for a different reason. Above all, he must not let the customer spill his guts. If he continues to be sore, the 9,1-oriented salesman is willing to move to the customer's side against his own company, saying perhaps, "Those bums—I'll raise hell when I get back to the factory, and get quick action to have this matter put right. In the meantime, don't worry about a thing." Salesman and customer have found accord by uniting against a third party.

Rush Business

The 9,1-minded salesman tends to be a "rush-business generator." Hooking a customer by promising earlier deliveries than he could normally expect, even when the salesman is pretty sure the factory can't handle it, is better than losing the order. He commits the factory on his own initiative and begins at once to turn his pressure onto Manufacturing to see to it that the delivery is made as promised. He may have ways of his own, back in the company, to get priority on his rush orders, even though the orders booked by other salesmen get delayed. This is just another indication of his low concern for people in general. His self-justification is, If you don't look out for Number One, who will?

INTEGRITY

Results are what count to the 9,1-oriented salesman. "The end justifies the means." His product is the best ever, and he'll go for broke to move it. Things are either good or bad, up or down, but never sideways, in the selling situation. To whatever question the customer raises, he gives the answer that sells. If the customer resists, the salesman increases the pressure, and often without his realizing it, some factual distortion creeps in.

The customer's reaction to the big 9,1 buildup can be either one of two things. One is that the customer may be just testing the salesman, asking questions that he already knows the answer to. If the salesman gives an incorrect reply under these circumstances, his goose is cooked. He loses the customer's confidence. The customer has proved to himself that he is right, and here's another of those lying, crooked salesmen. There's no way of gluing together the egg that has been cracked. The salesman has little chance of getting back into the customer's good graces—once a liar, always a liar. The other possibility is that the customer might not have sufficient background information to be able to detect the bias in the salesman's presentation. Nevertheless, customers can usually discern the over-simplified, black-or-white state-ment. Some are highly capable, once stimulated, of conducting an in-quisition which can become a win-lose battle, and the blood that gets spilled is not the customer's.

To a customer, who is "the other person" in this situation, integrity is a matter of the man's being consistent in what he says and what he does. It is seen when there is an unbroken connection between his spoken and actual behavior and when these both adhere to a code of high moral values. The issues of integrity come through clearly in connection with those promises which create firm expectations in the customer's mind. The matter of delivery promises, mentioned in the previous section, is an example of how some basic 9,1 attitudes show through. Having made a delivery commitment, and thereby obtaining the order, the salesman's conscience usually is satisfied by a brisk, "Now see here, you guys. . . ." message or pep talk to the production people concerning the urgency of this order. If they can't cut it, the customer can be told afterwards, when it's too late for him to back out, that he's going to have to wait a little while. The salesman is confident, if this happens, that he can hold on to him and repair any damage that has been done.

These kinds of factual distortions stretch the truth; they make it elastic. But this is not "lying" in the malicious sense of falsehood. The salesman may very well be convinced at the time he is giving the promise that what he is saying is truth itself. His attitude is that the key element in each statement is true, or at least is more true than untrue. In one sense it might be said that truth begins when the ele-ments in a selling presentation, taken as a whole, are 51 percent or more valid. Lying begins when less than 50 percent of the elements are accurate. In other words, if the majority of a statement is true, the whole is true, because the valid elements outweigh the invalid ones. So in his own view, the salesman is not being untrue if some elements, unverifiable but of lesser importance, are thrown in to supplement the main point he is getting across. This is what it is that permits the 9,1-oriented salesman to polarize his presentation in categorical terms of "all good" or "all bad." It allows him to oversimplify the issues and to leave things out which, in his view, are unimportant. As a result, the sheer strength of his convictions can be highly persuasive to himself and to others, because as far as he is concerned the exceptions or contradictions don't count.

SELF-MANAGEMENT

A 9,1-oriented salesman is inner-directed and keeps tight rein on himself. His inner gyroscope maintains his purposefulness in all situations. It can result in inflexible and rigid self-prescription which, in the extreme, can program him like a computer. Once his course is set, he finds it difficult to veer to either one side or the other. The positive aspect is that he is well organized and acts in a purposeful manner, not letting trivial or extraneous factors cause him to falter. The negative side is that he is too often blinded to the unforeseen opportunities that can become noticeable during an interview. When new information becomes available which he should interpret as the basis for redirecting himself, he is likely to brush it aside and continue on his way.

Time I plan a fixed schedule of activities several days in advance and do my best to avoid deviating from it. By having my activities well organized, I can use my time with customers to maximum advantage. I don't tolerate much disturbance in my schedule.

Prospecting I track down every prospect brought to my attention. No stone is left unturned. I push myself to make a specific number of new contacts, on a cold-canvassing basis, if necessary, every week.

Servicing Since I intend to sell him some more, the customer is the boss. I keep constant pressure on my company's internal organization to ensure that his service requirements are satisfied.

Expenses I am ready to answer for every penny I spend. The expenses I incur while with customers are a means to an end: getting increased sales. The expenses I incur for myself are in line with the effort I put out.

Self-steering I analyze the record of my ongoing sales results to make sure I'm keeping ahead. Some self-appraisal may be useful if failures occur, but for me it's diligent effort that makes for better performance.[10]

What is the probable impact of a 9,1 orientation on the profitability of selling? He might sum up his own attitudes in the following way: "By working hard and driving myself, I operate in the best interest of the company. Getting more and more business is the most important aspect of my job and that means increasing sales volume. Profit is the direct result." This "push the tons and profit dollars will result" mentality is the hallmark of 9,1 thinking. It is right in that dollars won't result unless the product moves. However, it may be very wrong, too, because the 9,1 way of selling, which undercuts competitors, can undercut profits too. It may move the product once but alienate the customer forever. It may get the sale but have such costly servicing consequences that no result would have been less damaging.

CUSTOMER REACTIONS

9,1 as a selling strategy can be very successful, no question about it. A reason is that the 9,1 salesman is a take-charge type of guy. He is likely to move fast, to exercise positive persuasion on the customer, to communicate his own enthusiasm for his product, and to brush aside objections as trivial and unimportant. In this way, a customer can be swept off his feet and into an impetuous buying decision.

What are the probable consequences of this kind of selling approach? First of all, the customer is likely to feel hemmed in, impressed by the benefits and unable to muster a statement of any reservations or doubts he may feel. Second, he may sense that the sales presentation, persuasive as it is, does not deal with any problem of his that a purchase might contribute to solving, but he has difficulty in knowing why. Third, if anything in the presentation goes counter to what he *does* know about the product—or thinks he knows about it—or if it opposes what he is sure he needs, resentment and hostility are likely to build up.

Thus a hard-driving approach is likely to have one of two results. One is that it will bring about submission even though disguised resentment may be present. The salesman, meeting no resistance, proceeds swiftly through his presentation and then presses the customer to buy. He may do so, and it is also possible that he will not be dissatisfied with the product later on. But if he *is* subsequently disappointed with his purchase, he is likely to recall how he was rushed into buying it, and he will make a mental note to stay clear of this salesman in the future.

The other reaction is that the 9,1 approach may promote active hostility on the part of the prospect. If this happens, the salesman quickly finds himself in a no-win situation. Objection after objection is thrown up, no one of which is the real reason for reluctance, but the unexpressed attitude is, "I'll be damned if I'll buy from this s.o.b." The 9,1 way of pressuring to close a sale often heightens customer resistance rather than reducing it. The reason is that the customer senses that the salesman's objective is to make a sale rather than to supply what he, the customer, desires.

A number of consequences of the 9,1 approach can be anticipated, depending on the customer's Grid style. The 9,1 exploitative kind of purchaser will recognize immediately that here is a salesman who means to do him in, and he is likely to respond with open hostility and resentment. Discussion quickly moves into a win-lose fight. Sometimes the salesman may win a sale if, during the argument, the customer wins some of his points and thereby convinces himself that he is wringing a good bargain from the salesman. About equally as often there is a standoff, and no sale is made.

If the customer's style is 1,9, he may respond with submission and acquiescence as though to avoid offending the 9,1-oriented salesman. The inert 1,1 customer may be expected to go along if there is an obvious fit between the product, as the salesman describes it, and a need that he has. If he is a company purchasing agent, he can be swayed by the 9,1 presentation if the product meets the criteria set by his boss. If the product does not fit his buying specifications, he is likely to defer making a decision, to procrastinate indefinitely. If this path of retreat is cut off by the salesman's tight closing maneuvers, the customer might evince an unexpectedly strong backup and even fight with the ferocity of a "natural" 9,1.

A 5,5 customer is susceptible to a 9,1 approach as long as the salesman's presentation strikes the right harmonies in appealing to what he values highly—the product's prestige as demonstrated by the fact that a number of illustrious people or companies are using or at least endorsing it. If not immediately convinced on the basis of product reputation, he can become very choosy. Much depends on the salesman's treatment of his inquiries, as to whether he will eventually purchase or not.

The 9,9 objective-minded purchaser may be expected to react with impatience to the nonfactual and irrelevant emphases in the hard-sell presentation and only to buy after satisfying himself fully that the product precisely matches his requirement. In this kind of situation, there is a strong likelihood that the customer will exercise leadership and provoke the salesman into being more factual and precise in what he says about the product. In effect, he is making it necessary for the salesman to shift into a 9,9 backup as the basis on which he can have a satisfactory sales interview with the customer who is oriented in this way.

chapter five

1,9

1,9 AS A SALES STYLE strongly reflects an individual's concern for the way he is being reacted to by others. He is responsive to other people. He wants to be liked by them and to gain their approval of whatever he is doing or saying. So what they are currently thinking about him and whether this indicates acceptance or rejection of him in personal terms are most important. He is sensitive to what he detects as movement either way. Thus the basic motivation of the person who is oriented in a 1,9 fashion is to gain acceptance, sometimes regardless of the personal effort and the degree of acquiescence involved. He puts a high value on good relationships, on being a "nice guy." He worries about how people are feeling. A customer's frown is a bad sign; a smile means the interview is going well. When a discussion is over, he is more likely to give an account of the emotions that he felt in the situation, and the nuances of interaction, than of the logic and flow of the ideas that were presented.

To avoid being rejected himself, he tries to avoid giving any impression that he is rejecting anyone. How is this done? One way is by embracing the opinions, attitudes, and ideas of others in preference to forwarding his own. This does two things. It permits him to agree with others, and it also reduces the possibility that others will disagree with him. As a result, when he expresses convictions, these are more likely to be reflections of what his boss or his colleagues or his customers think and want than something that he has thought through for himself and founded his own beliefs upon. He is a good listener and is inclined to encourage others in what they are proposing, regardless of validity or soundness.

As far as ideas and programs of action go, he is a follower. But he does actively initiate contacts, moving in to establish bonds of friendship and to create an atmosphere of congeniality. He rarely generates conflict, but when it does appear, either between himself and others, or between others, he tries to soothe bad feelings. His attribute of looking on the bright side has a quality of "Wanting will make it so," in contrast with the optimistic "Can do!" attitude of a person who sets his course of action and then works to bring it about. When there are tensions between people, his humor is aimed at reducing them and lightening the atmosphere. Because of his strong desire to avoid a stressful situation, it's sometimes difficult to maintain a serious-minded orientation under a situation of genuine concern when a 1,9-oriented person is about. His temper, in the sense of lashing out at others, is not easily triggered. Emotions of anger and hostility in others tend to increase his anxiety and solicitude. 1,9 is a friendly, likable orientation. *He is other-directed.* In contrast with 9,1, he takes his cues from *outside*, not from inside the person.

KNOWLEDGE: CUSTOMER, COMPETITOR, AND PRODUCT

With his characteristic high concern for people, a 1,9-oriented salesman has an active interest in developing his knowledge of the customer as a person. Where possible, he does some research on his prospect in advance to find out what sort of person he is and to look for conversational lead-ins that will promote friendly discussion with him. When meeting with a customer, he finds genuine interest in hearing about the other person's thoughts, attitudes, and opinions.

This interest does not limit itself to business matters. To know his hobbies, his family, the progress of his children in school, as well as his career aspirations, is a pleasure in itself to the salesman as well as part of his strategy for strengthening the bond with his customer. Through his many acquaintances he is attuned to a widely ranging network of hearsay, rumor, and gossip. He enjoys passing on his news and hearing the latest from the customers and others with whom he has established amicable relationships. A salesman with 1,9 attitudes often will significantly increase sales costs by insisting on paying for meals, drinks, and entertainment. His rationale is sound to him—it builds friendship. He also is easily influenced by a 9,1-oriented customer to urge his company to give quantity discounts or other price concessions which might be unwarranted when related to manufacturing costs and the current market situation.

A 1,9-oriented salesman is unlikely to develop deep knowledge and understanding of his company's competitors. There are more agreeable things to think about. The attitude of businesslike vigilance, so essential for becoming aware and informed about competitors, does not square with the 1,9 view of the world. To him, competition is a form of conflict—something unpleasant; he does not concern himself with it. So this salesman has a blind spot, and a frequent result is that he is taken unawares.

The desire to be liked by one and all leads the salesman with a 1,9 attitude to be complimentary about competitors in a way that can be very disquieting to the customer. This is not to say, of course, that the salesman bursts forth with spontaneous praise of competitors, but that his basic attitude is, "Don't say anything unless you can say something pleasant." When invited to comment on a competitor's product, the salesman's response is to avoid saying anything that might be interpreted as critical and to be generous in his remarks. There is, of course, a likelihood that the salesman's compliments and warm attitudes may enhance the competitor's product in the eyes of the prospect and thereby make what the salesman himself is presenting less attractive. But if the customer probes beneath these compliments and discovers that the salesman is actually deficient in his understanding of the competitor whom he complimented—unaware of his sales strategies, products, pricing, and so on—the salesman's credibility is reduced.

The salesman's knowledge of his own product tends to be superficial. He is more likely to be able to recount features that appeal to the senses than to give a technical explanation of "how it works." Knowledge is a means to an end rather than an end in itself. To be helpful, he learns what it is that customers *want* to know rather than what it is they *need* to know as a basis for making sound purchase decisions. He does keep a ready store of amusing anecdotes relating to the product and its users which can stimulate an interest or positive reaction. The fact that people like the product is more compelling to him than how they *use* it.

PARTICIPATION AND INVOLVEMENT

A salesman with a 1,9 orientation has a concept of two people—the customer and himself—getting together in a congenial relationship. This is his idea of participation and involvement. When people like one another, it is easy to do business together. And he has found his vocation—he is being paid to make friends.

Listening is important. He would never think of preventing the customer from expressing himself. He is ready to listen to whatever the customer wants to talk about, and whenever the conversation lags, he will find a new topic to keep it going. What this may do, in fact, is to help relax the customer and maybe influence him to see the salesman as a pleasant person with whom to do business.

But the discussion has a "pseudo" quality. It is congenial, unhurried, and sociable, yet it probably does very little to create a suitable atmosphere for a business transaction. It is more in the nature of a coffee-break visit. It is not the kind of involvement that begins to heighten the customer's interest in the product. The salesman's characteristic approach, the very assumptions under which he conducts himself, causes him to hold back from any kind of guiding initiative toward "getting down to cases" concerning the product.

Some customers are pleased to see their 1,9 friend when he comes to call. After an enjoyable chat on current events, the friend may indicate that he has something interesting to show him. If it is the brochure of a high-priced equipment item, the customer is likely to remark, "That's really interesting, Tom. Leave it with me and I'll take a look through it and discuss it with our technical people." They lapse back into irrelevant conversation, and eventually Tom takes his leave with a smile and a handshake. The customer thinks, "Nice guy, that Tom. Good to have him stop by, but gee, it's getting late." He writes a colleague's name on the brochure and puts it into his "out" box, and that is the last that is ever heard of it.

At other times Tom may come in with a fairly low-priced novel item, and the customer in a similar good mood says, "They're great little gadgets. I'll take a couple right away." Tom is delighted. His theory is borne out—a sale is made. Maybe, though, if he had probed to find out from his friend the objective needs of the company that the product could satisfy, he could have sold a couple of gross.

Other customers are not so chummy these days. "Oh, you're here again, Tom. You've caught me between two appointments. We've got just three minutes at the outside, so what is it today?" Busy people prefer to participate and involve themselves in profitable and productive activities.

Warm-up

The initial step for a 1,9 salesman is to get acquainted with the customer. He wants to establish a comfortable atmosphere and to feel secure that the customer accepts him as a person. The 1,9 assumption is that people will usually do business with those they like. He may talk and joke with the customer until he is relaxed and in a receptive mood. The salesman uses flattery in a spontaneous way, finding something in the person or his organization to single out for favorable comments. Then the conversation turns to the prospect's personal interests. This gives him the opportunity to make a friend and creates a climate where unpleasant issues are unlikely to arise. The salesman possesses an endless reservoir of small talk and often will leave it to the customer to initiate the shift from social chat to the sales interview.

Sales Presentation

In his discussion about the product, the 1,9-oriented salesman suggests what is attractive about it and what some of the features are that the customer might like.

He will usually begin in a tentative way, describing a number of "interesting" and maybe novel features. These are conversational appetizers to induce the client to express a favorable opinion or to mention what feature of the product he finds appealing. The 1,9 salesman is gun-shy about expressing any opinion of his own until he has "read the signs" from the other person. As soon as the customer expresses an opinion, the salesman reinforces these inclinations if they are favorable. He compliments the customer's good taste and adds to it by agreeing that he likes that feature too. If the customer's expressed opinion is unfavorable to the product, he cushions its impact by implicitly yielding the point and perhaps even apologizing. Then he moves on to another positive product feature. Under the 1,9 convention of "Don't say anything unless you can say something favorable," any product features that might not be so attractive from the customer's point of view are ignored or glossed over, not because of a desire to win (in contrast to 9,1), but to keep the visit a friendly one. By the same token, criticism of competitor products is avoided as well.

Objections

How does a salesman with 1,9 assumptions deal with disagreement and conflict? On the emotional side, he would see an objection as a breach in the harmony that he is trying to establish. He would usually try to steer the conversation away from topics that might provoke controversy and ill feelings. But if an objection does arise, he tries to smooth it over. He may avoid answering the objection by saying, "It's not important," or "Let's set this one aside for a moment; we can work it out later on." He might bypass the objection by yielding to the customer's point. Or he may shift the conversation by telling a joke that will ease his own tensions and the customer's as well.

If he does not possess enough detailed product knowledge to give a specific answer to the objection, he is likely to give a global one which envelops the query but does not answer it. Another thought characteristic of a 1,9-oriented person is to take a specific point and enlarge it, or a concrete position and abstract from it to a plane of generalization where everyone can agree and be *for*. In this way he is as much a master of the tactics of depolarization as the 9,1 is of polarization.

All of these responses blur an objection and make the limitation that the customer wished to discuss appear less critical. It's nearly impossible to get an argument going! But the objections which have been deflected in these ways may work against the possibility of making a sale, particularly when the customer becomes so suspicious that his unanswered objection gets magnified out of proportion to its true importance.

Closing

The salesman with 1,9 assumptions worries that he may throw the customer off balance if he exerts selling pressure. His anxiety is that the customer may say No. Unlike the 9,1-oriented salesman who is likely to be deaf to No, his antenna is delicately tuned to this possibility. He prefers to refrain from pushing the customer for a declaration so as not to risk an outright turn-down. In this way he hangs back, waiting for the customer to make a spontaneous buying decision. If this does not come, he is quite willing to acquiesce in the face of procrastination or indecisiveness. He invites the customer to think about it and to keep in touch with him. At the same time, he indicates his pleasure and appreciation at having had the opportunity to visit with him.

If the customer already has doubts about the wisdom of making a purchase, this lack of a positive attitude on the salesman's part is only likely to expand it. The reason is that a customer usually takes for granted that the salesman has a positive regard for his own product. Thus, he often expects and is listening for the salesman to come up with a decisive reason why he ought to purchase it right away.

ESTABLISHED BUSINESS

The salesman spends a lot of time with the customers he likes. He enjoys their company and his easygoing relationship with them.

Maintaining Accounts

He tells himself that social contacts are necessary. He is Johnny-on-the-spot, and any business will naturally fall his way. In this way he rationalizes his excessive expenditure of nonproductive time. He is less keen about visiting those of his established accounts who tend to be abrupt and abrasive with him. Because their harsh attitudes make him shun their presence, they are open targets for competitors. As the fractures in the relationship become wider, leading to the extinction of the account, he interprets this as lack of interest in buying.

Complaints

Complaints from a customer raise a 1,9 salesman's anxieties. He dreads facing a customer who is angry or frustrated. This causes him to delay or put off meeting him head on. When he does, he shows his concern by being very apologetic. He lets the customer know that it hurts him too. Through this kind of joint commiseration, they may begin to get back on a friendly basis. Sometimes the salesman's regret at the inconvenience caused to the customer makes him promise more in restitution than can really be accomplished by the supplying company. Meanwhile, as a personal gesture of apology, the salesman goes out of his way to do a special favor for the customer as soon as possible.

Rush Business

So as to avoid the customer displeasure that would ensue if he said No, the salesman will readily promise to do everything he can to get the rush business through. To keep out of trouble with his own company's operations people, he lets them know that he always tries to keep unnecessary demands to a minimum. This inconsistency is examined in the next section.

INTEGRITY

The salesman who operates from 1,9 assumptions is a hopeful optimist. Everything should turn out all right. There is no need to paint anything but the brightest picture. This may involve him in misrepresentation at times. The 1,9 attitude toward truth can be understood when it is recognized that his wishes and desires tend to get mixed up with data and facts. He wants to keep that customer happy all through the interview. The possibility that the customer may become very unhappy later on with what he has purchased is, at present, only a small cloud on the horizon.

He finds truth in what he wishes or hopes for at the moment when he speaks. If a customer states a number of requirements and asks whether the product meets them, the salesman remains more interested in staying personally acceptable than in satisfying the requirements specified. If the salesman senses that some specifications cannot be met, he "emphasizes the positive." If he can't "eliminate the negative," he apologizes. Worse, he may hastily reply to a customer, "Yes, I'm sure it will meet all your requirements," without running a mental check on the possibilities that it may not.

Like the 9,1-oriented salesman, he may enter into commitments to the customer that have little prospect of being fulfilled. But the way of doing it differs. This can be illustrated in the delivery-promise situation. While the 9,1 salesman, carried along by the force of his conviction that this is how it's *got* to be, may say, "It'll be here at 9 A.M. Thursday," the hope-charged 1,9 statement is likely to be, "I'll do everything I can to meet your request. I am sure we can have it delivered for you on Thursday." At the moment he says this, he wants so much to meet the customer's desire that he feels there has to be truth in what he is saying. And he will ask the factory production manager—as a personal favor to him—to try to speed the order through. They are all good men and will do their best. Only later, when the facts loom so large, does he realize that he has entered into unreal commitments. He is wistful. He was not really being untrue; he felt so sure at the time. Knowing how disappointed the customer will be when the delivery is not made on schedule, the salesman will try to persuade him into being patient—even in advance of the event. He is very contrite and apologetic. "So many unexpected difficulties are cropping up, but we are doing everything possible. Really, we feel so badly about disappointing you. . . ."

And so it goes on. His desire to be helpful always tips the balance over his ability to maintain a realistically objective awareness of what can be done. The effect on the customer of the 1,9 optimistic head-in-the-clouds statement is likely to be that he accepts it the first time, but once the pattern becomes evident, the customer quickly turns off and avoids the warm salesman on whom he cannot rely.

SELF-MANAGEMENT

A salesman who is oriented in a 1,9 way tends to be managed by others rather than to "manage" himself. He is not a self-regulator in planning, scheduling, and organizing himself at the detail level. He is a responder. In this sense, he is directed from outside himself by whoever exercises influence—the customer, the sales manager, family, and friends. Not every influence from the outside has a magnetic effect. Rather, he is drawn to those influences that are positive and repelled by those that are not.

> **Time**   I am at the disposal of my customers. My work schedule has flexibility so that I can help my customers when they need me.
>
> **Prospecting**   When an indication of positive interest has been shown, I follow up. I ask the customers with whom I have a good relationship for suggestions concerning new people to contact.
>
> **Servicing**   I visit with the customer and am happy when I can provide a requested service, even one that is beyond his expectations of what we should contribute. Nothing is too good for our customers.
>
> **Expenses**   I need a reasonable expense account to carry out my job. If I spend beyond the policy limit, it's because I feel I am serving the company through promoting customer goodwill. To a large extent, business is built on my ability to present myself in a pleasing manner and under pleasant circumstances.
>
> **Self-steering**   I am wide awake to how others react to me and to what I do that increases my acceptance by them. A good personality is what sells products and services.[11]

What is the 1,9 impact on profitable selling? This attitude is, "Profit is desirable but should not be the key factor when good customer relationships are at stake. I prefer a customer whose business is easy to handle and good for the company." He clearly puts people ahead of profit. This is the great risk that he creates. If he pursues his own inclinations, he sells but not very frequently at a high volume for a sustained period of time with a particular account. He is likely to bring about closings that, in the long term, are costly to the company rather than making a significant profit contribution.

CUSTOMER REACTIONS

In contrast with the way in which a 9,1-oriented salesman tries to force his customers into buying decisions, the salesman who operates under 1,9 is likely to follow the customer, adjusting his own pace to the other's tempo. He is unlikely to take one of the customer's proposals and shift into an alternative way of thinking, as the customer might not like it. He thinks this might provoke backlash. His way is to listen keenly for positive customer attitudes toward features of his product and then to add his constructive support to what has been said. This way, he can avoid provoking objections while continuing to add support and encouragement to the customer's "buy attitude," such as it is.[12]

The 1,9 sales presentation is most successful when made to a sociable 1,9 customer, because the needs of each to be liked by the other are consummated in a purchase.

The 1,1 customer, feeling little impact from a 1,9 presentation, finds it relatively easy to give a noncommittal answer and so escape, or to disengage by indicating his lack of interest.

A 5,5 customer might buy if he clearly recognized that he had a need for the product and was assured that everyone who had bought it was satisfied with it.

A 9,9 customer is likely to feel impatient with the irrelevancy and "soft touch" qualities—the lack of solid fact—which characterizes the 1,9 sales presentation. He defers further consideration until provided with more straightforward product information.

When the customer is 9,1, the salesman is likely to buckle quickly under the pressure of forceful criticism, closing his briefcase and thanking the customer for the favor of granting him time.

chapter six

1,1

THE SALESMAN WHO has adopted a 1,1 orientation is committed neither to mastering the environment in which he works nor to being admired by the people in it. He is turned inward and encased there. Survival within the business system he represents is his dominant concern. His level of personal satisfaction is that of "feeling no pain." It has become his state of adjustment. He moves along paths of least resistance, going through the expected motions without convictions or personal warmth. Somehow he has lost enthusiasm for selling, but he has to keep his job. So he trudges around, making some minimum quota of sales calls, or stands behind a counter, immobile as a statue.

This withdrawal into himself, with the consequent lack of conviction about the job he should be doing, shows through clearly to customers and others. It is a generalized indifference both to them and to the product or service with which he is associated. He will not involve himself in the customer's problems of choice. His view is, "That's up to him." He is governed by the principle of least effort and does not tamper with the circumstances that he finds himself in. He gives no more than token support to his product and rarely expresses any point of view. His mental energy is low. He seems colorless, devoid of feeling. This has a deadening effect, even on hostile customers—there is no response even if someone is trying to pick a fight with him. He just crouches in his mental foxhole, and the verbal bullets fly over his head. His emotions are not engaged, so he rarely gets stirred up. Alternative ways of viewing the situation do not arise spontaneously from within, nor is he likely to be stimulated or challenged from without. He seldom exhibits humor, or if he does, it is likely to be seen by others as rather pointless.

The 1,1 approach is *nondirected*. From the outside, one can detect little or no evidence of any active pursuit of a path of interest or achievement. Rather, the behavior is more like that of a jellyfish which floats, responding to the motion of the waves without moving in any direction of its own.

The notion of a person, in a selling context, having both a low concern for customers and a low concern for making a sale may at first glance seem improbable. Yet on deeper reflection you will find that you can recall individuals who have adopted this orientation. Because they make no dramatic splash and do not stir up trouble, they can become nearly invisible, particularly in a situation of low competition and high demand.

The salesman with a 1,1 orientation has learned to be "out of it" while remaining in the organization. As a dominant style, it is an unnatural approach. It is one a man is likely to adopt or slowly slide into when he personally accepts defeat. He may have lost confidence in the product he represents, feeling that there is no real hope of selling it against the competitors' lines. Possibly he has become discouraged by some buyers' attitudes toward him as a salesman and thinks he is trapped in a job that lacks status. To permit himself to become involved and concerned over what happens in the selling situation can only lead him to deeper frustration and discouragement. As a backup or temporary standby style, it is not uncommon, and many salesmen can readily identify the pressures under which they are likely to "go 1,1."

KNOWLEDGE: PRODUCT, CUSTOMER, OR COMPETITOR

A salesman with dominant 1,1 attitudes is not interested in gaining any more than a routine knowledge of his product. If questioned closely about the product's features, he might reply, "I only know the general details. It's hard for a salesman to keep up with all the complexity in our products nowadays. You can get in touch with our technical people if you are interested." The most he can do during the sales interview is bring out a book of technical specifications or read from the product brochure. He rarely initiates a discussion of the product's applicability in terms of how the customer might use it to fulfill his own particular requirements.

Much the same attitude toward knowledge is found in the area of understanding a customer. He has little interest in him as a person. He sees no reason why he should bother to reconnoiter the customer's situation. Once the product has been described, the customer—who knows his situation best—can use his own background information to test whether or not he needs it. He's going to make up his own mind in the end anyway.

The salesman probably realizes that active competitors can cut down his sales volume, but he feels there is little he can do about it. Casing the competitors to get to know more about them and their products is not going to change them or make a dime's worth of difference either way. "Why worry? It's better to ignore them."

A customer may want to pose questions concerning the relative merits of the product which the salesman is presenting and those of competitors. An ignorant or uninformed salesman leaves the customer unsatisfied when he is unable to field such inquiries. Additionally, his actual void of information makes it impossible for him to correct any false impressions that may have been put into the customer's mind by a competitor.

PARTICIPATION AND INVOLVEMENT

The 1,1 attitude produces little desire to promote a give-and-take interaction with a customer and involve him in discussions. "If the prospect wants it, he'll buy it. If he doesn't, he won't—and there's not much you can do about it. I provide some information, and the next move's up to him."

Unlike the target of a 9,1 approach, the customer has an unlimited opportunity to talk. However, if he is sensitive to the quality of silence, he is unlikely to feel that he is being genuinely listened to by the 1,1-oriented salesman.

It is an odd experience to be visited by a salesman who has adopted the bombed-out 1,1 approach, maybe as a result of repeated failures and disillusion. He sits down, dead pan, and speaks briefly, with no enthusiasm. You have an eerie feeling that a prerecorded announcement is being played over and transmitted somehow from a human voice-box. The message doesn't grab you in the least, but maybe you see some use for the product and you pose some inquiries about it. Again, and even more intensely, you have the feeling that you are hooked up to a telephone answering service. The answers surprise you at first by their lack of connection with the question you asked. Then you become aware that you are not going to get a precise answer at all. This machine's not equipped to give one. Perhaps he promises to refer your question to someone else, more technically qualified than he is, who will get in touch with you in due course.

He asks you, "Would you like to place an order in the meantime?"

You say, "No."

"Well, that's okay, I'll call again sometime." And he flits.

Mr. 1,1's visit has reminded you that you could make use of some particular item. He *has* involved you, but not to his own company's benefit. Other suppliers are listed in the directory; you make a telephone call—on a live line this time. One of their salesmen stops by. You check out a comparable product to your own satisfaction and order it.

Opening

The salesman's attitude toward prospects is based on thoughts such as these: "When making the first contact it would be a waste of effort to do any more than describe the product, giving the basic facts"; "If the guy wants to know something, he'll ask"; "There's no sense in trying to probe the customer's thinking—he's probably made up his mind already." So without further ado he usually goes straight into his sales presentation without bothering to explore whether or not he has the customer's interest and attention.

Sales Presentation

A 1,1 presentation is likely to be mighty sparse, unembroidered, and threadbare. Having a low concern for making a sale as well as for the customer's needs, the salesman's job, as he sees it, is to let the customer know that the product is available and to give a brief description of it. Thus, he is as unlikely to promote the product's positive features as he is to volunteer any information concerning the limits of its performance capability. His basic strategy is to go through the motions, giving a low-keyed pitch and without making any effort to relate the product's characteristics to the customer's situation. He can provide only perfunctory answers to a customer's requests for information. Like the 1,9 approach, but for a different reason, the 1,1 sales presentation also abstains from knocking competitors and their products. "Why take the trouble?"

Objections

The 1,1-oriented salesman may, like his 1,9 counterpart, try to steer the conversation along an objection-free path, his particular reason being that this is the easiest way to handle the interview. Once an objection is raised, his strategy is either to ignore it or to imply that he goes along with it for what it's worth. As far as possible, he sees no disagreement, hears no disagreement, and speaks no disagreement. As a matter of fact, he's also likely to *feel* no disagreement, since neutrality is at his emotional core. The calm, placid, patient exterior is not from inner peace but from being devoid of emotional involvement and thus untouched by a challenge, contradiction, or hostile attack.

If he gets caught up and drawn back to facing the objection, he will most probably try to downplay the objection by saying that the problem is unlikely to arise. Or he may divert the conversation by indicating that he would have to consult with someone back at the company to get a detailed answer to this "technical" question. When asked what people think about a product or a problem, he possesses an infinite variety of neutral answers, "They didn't say"; "I haven't heard"; "I wasn't there." When pressed for his recommendation or conviction, he is equally adept, "It's up to you"; "I wouldn't want to influence your decisions"; "Whatever you say"; "I'm no expert. . . ." If he is slick with words, he may try to double-talk the customer, creating a mirage of words—an answer that is not an answer. "It could be X . . . for the following reasons . . . or it could be Y . . . but I'm not sure which is best." In all these ways the 1,1 salesman evades being drawn into disagreement and controversy. When there is a choice between dealing fully with the customer's objection or losing the sale, he'd rather lose the sale.

Closing

The salesman approaches the closing phase of the interview in a very matter-of-fact way. His closing initiative may be little more than a vague question, Do you feel like buying it? If the customer wants it, fine. He is ready to take the order. In this sense he can be viewed as a message carrier. He more or less mechanically transmits the customer's purchase order to his own company for processing without adding energy of his own.

If the decision is not to buy, well okay. "You can't win them all." To this salesman it is obvious that the customer had no interest to begin with, so why should he waste time beating a dead horse? Even if the customer had shown some interest but is still undecided, the salesman accepts the first No he gets. To him it is axiomatic that prospects rarely want to do business on the first contact. They have to mull things over. He indicates where he can be reached if needed, then departs.

ESTABLISHED BUSINESS

Steady customers are what the salesman relies upon for his bread and butter. By moving around his traditional circuit he can take their periodic orders without even raising a sweat.

Maintaining Accounts

The salesman with a 1,1 orientation tends to gravitate to situations where regular customers can provide him with sufficient income. Usually, he can maintain a stable sales volume under these circumstances, and as long as the company's satisfied, so is he. This kind of reliable timetable for contacting established accounts and collecting their orders with minimum intrusion can be quite acceptable to the habitual customer too. It does not burden him with making new decisions. Neither does it occupy his time in listening to the kind of sales talk that he has heard previously.

The circumstance where a salesman has generated a large number of established accounts, who are unlikely to take their business elsewhere, coupled with a generous income deriving from his initial efforts to generate these customers, can make it easy for a salesman to slide from some other orientation into a 1,1 attitude. He doesn't have to scramble for customers. His income is already beyond his earlier expectations. He can be lulled into inactivity without realizing it, and the company suffers.

Complaints

Complaints are inevitable. A salesman with 1,1 attitudes has developed ways to insulate himself from being stirred up by them or becoming involved in putting things right. He feels no personal responsibility for the difficulty. Generally he functions as a message carrier by saying, "I'll pass that along to the plant and somebody will let you know." He may say to himself, "There's nothing I can do about it; let somebody else get the grief."

If the customer persists with the complaint, the salesman will say, "Look, put that in writing, will you? I'll see that it gets to the right people." He himself will do nothing, on the assumption that if he stays out of it, "nature will take its course." Since the salesman does not get aroused or anxious about the complaint, it may eventually come to appear unimportant in the customer's eyes as well! If subsequently the customer presses for action, the salesman says, "I'll follow up on it," but probably does nothing, on the assumption that if he waits long enough the problem will go away. Sometimes this actually happens.

Rush Business

The 1,1 attitude is that rush business is risky business. The difficulties encountered in trying to satisfy it are, as often as not, greater than the gain in sales volume to be had from it. The salesman is likely to suggest to the customer that there is no real need for this degree of urgency, and that he, the customer, is sure to find ways of getting along until a normal delivery can be made. The salesman defers taking the order and thereby avoids accepting a potentially worrisome responsibility. Others' problems are not his worries, but if necessary he'll agree to the go-between role and relay the request and answer from customer to company and back again.

INTEGRITY

The 1,1 attitude toward integrity has a reverse twist in it. To avoid any future charge that he has misrepresented the product or broken a promise, he *underpromises*, preferring to lose an order than to get into the crack or out on a limb. Thus, he retains a kind of passive integrity. For safety's sake, he may draw back from making some commitment that is well within his, the product's, or his company's capability to perform. "I don't know whether we can guarantee that, I'd have to get someone to check it out. Is it important? . . . Oh well, maybe you could ask your engineers what they think. Here are the specifications." He now has his alibi ready for the future. But the reaction of a customer to the 1,1, "I don't know" is likely to be a loss of respect because the salesman cannot relieve blockages, such as late deliveries, that are preventing progress.

Again, even when he knows that delivery may be possible by Thursday, though not likely under the usual delivery routine, he will say it can't be done before the following Monday at the earliest. In this way, he avoids any risk that he might be wrong and violate the customer's expectations, while in fact, not playing it straight with him. If a piece of information turns up which the salesman did not volunteer and he is queried about it, his response is, "But you didn't ask about *that*," shifting the blame off his shoulders onto another.

SELF-MANAGEMENT

A 1,1-oriented salesman tends to be inert, only increasing his tempo or shifting direction when a crisis hits. Since he is only marking time within the system, he is not stimulated to do more than what is required of him. His mind is not in gear.

Time   I don't need to schedule my activities. Customers contact me, and their requests keep me busy enough.

Prospecting   I rely mostly on prospects contacting me. When I get time, I follow up on ones that are pointed out.

Servicing   The business is out of my hands once it reaches the office. The customer will let me know if there is anything else he needs from us. When he does, I'll pass the message on.

Expenses   I know how my expenses run. I stay in line.

Self-steering   I feel no need to review my performance. The boss will tell me what I need to know.[13]

What is the likely impact on profit of a 1,1-oriented salesman? His attitude is, "I accept the business that comes my way. This is my job; I guess all business is profitable." In fact, he is likely to lose more customers than he gains and to have a decreasing sales volume over time. Given a really competitive selling situation, then, he constitutes dead weight—carried by the organization but not contributing to it. It can be a case of all drag and no thrust.

CUSTOMER REACTIONS

Unless the customer has a burning desire to buy, or happens to be replenishing his inventory at the time the salesman visits him, it is unlikely that the 1,1 approach will result in pickup.

The salesman's pace is sluggish, frequently immobile. He remains in place, as passively as an automat, for the customer to make up his own mind about the purchase. One major difference between 1,1 and 1,9 is that if the customer expresses a positive attitude, the 1,1 salesman is unlikely to react to it. He gives no encouragement. Rather, he lets the remarks go by on the assumption that little can be done from outside to influence the customer's decision on a purchase. By the close of the interview he has done little to promote conviction, even less to arouse enthusiasm, and nothing to stimulate a customer's appreciation of the product.

The 1,1 sales strategy is unlikely to be effective with customers, whatever their Grid style, except where a clearly defined product need can be satisfied and when no other salesmen are promoting alternative products through which this need can be met; or where for some reason an established account has turned into a captive account.

The description above is of 1,1 as a dominant approach. Yet many a salesman, who is not uninvolved and unconcerned, can have 1,1 as a backup style or as a temporary response. A 1,1 retreat can occur when a person sees no available action to take to overcome an obstacle or barrier to a sale. Then he is likely to throw up his hands, saying to himself, "I don't care," and mentally or physically retire from the situation. He has become depressed by what he sees as customers' indifference toward him and their implicit rejection of him by not making purchases.[14] Or he may be caught in a win-lose fight, where his convictions are initially strong. Failing to prove his point but remaining unconvinced by his protagonist, he submits in defeat. He does not change his mind but withdraws energy and conviction under the emotion of, "It doesn't really matter anyway. There are more important things to do," or, "It's his decision even though I don't agree."

As a salesman who meets barriers and obstacles daily and perhaps hourly, the issue is to be alert to signs of easy recourse to a 1,1 attitude when the path to a sale is not a smooth one. Frequently, trying alternative ways of viewing a customer's problem, searching for more information from him to stimulate different ideas, summarizing so as to find whether an apparent impasse is a real one, or digging more deeply into the feelings that are being expressed beneath the words—plus other sound ways to maintain a problem-solving orientation—can lead to a successful interview.

chapter seven

5,5

The salesman with a 5,5 predisposition does not aim for a high degree of excellence in performance. Nor does he expect to build up ideal relationships with customers. He knows it is impractical to try for utopia, because no matter how hard you try, you can only please some of the customers some of the time. He prides himself on having a realistic outlook and on being a good steady performer who sets and reaches attainable sales objectives. He is not hitched to a star of hope. When he entered the selling profession, he may have read several handbooks or taken courses to find out which were the best selling methods founded on long experience—methods he could safely adopt. He has put these principles and techniques into action, modifying them where necessary to fit his own personal characteristics and the traditions of his company, and has developed them into a smooth tried-and-true selling technique of his own. Or maybe he relies on a company sales manual which recommends methods to be followed.

Generally his behavior is predictable. Whenever disagreements arise between him and his customers, he searches for compromise positions that can break the impasse. He tries to be fair and to get a resolution that is acceptable to each of the parties involved. He balances as many different considerations as he can in order to reach an appropriate compromise between inconsistent facts or conflicting views.

When operating on this basis of conventional practice, the 5,5-oriented salesman feels self-confident and ready to handle his customer. He can take the lead when precedents or past practices dictate the way. But he rarely modifies his standard selling technique or moves ahead of current trends in his company until a new direction has become well established. When he does introduce humor into a situation, it is of the persuasive kind that either sells himself in terms of increasing his acceptance by others or advances the point of view that he is taking.

It appears that most 5,5 motivations center on building up prestige and avoiding the shame that would come from its loss. Prestige, in this sense, has to do with a salesman's feeling himself to be valued by others for his own performance. He wants to be a good salesman in the eyes of his customers and in the estimation of his superiors and colleagues in the company. By respecting corporate traditions and norms, supporting the status quo, and avoiding behavior that might be viewed as deviating from established practices, this salesman gains a solid reputation. This and his predictably "sound" behavior—he believes—can steer him along a career path to security.

KNOWLEDGE: PRODUCT, COMPETITOR, AND CUSTOMER

Product knowledge is an important selling tool for a 5,5-oriented salesman. Yet his emphasis in gaining knowledge is to put himself in a position to deal satisfactorily with the most frequent customer inquiries. He knows something about everything but not a very great deal about anything. He prepares himself to talk about the main features and functions of the product but does not think it important to be able to deal with technical aspects and matters of detail in the way that an expert might. He can put the information over in a way that convinces most of the customers that he knows his product. But usually his knowledge is not detailed enough to be a basis for his suggesting new and creative ways in which the product can be used by customers. Thus he can cope with questions as to how his product will fit standard situations, but he is either not keen to venture outside his area or unable to see outside it. For example, if he is selling a small pocket-size camera, he will give a good account of its hobby uses, but it will probably not occur to him that the camera can be useful too in business and industrial applications such as making a photographic record of production charts before the entries are changed.

Before contacting new business prospects, he tries to establish some knowledge of them. The type of information he seeks is what positions they hold in their organizations and their relative status, where they went to school, and what is their standing in the community. These kinds of data are sufficient for the purpose of getting on terms with the customer in the opening stage of the interview. However, these data are not enough for readying the salesman for the customer's problems and the ways in which the product might provide a solution to them. The salesman has a well-marshalled list (sometimes supplied by his company) of high-status product users who can always be referred to by name and quoted favorably during an interview as the basis for building a new prospect's confidence. He sees name-dropping as one of his primary tools of influence.

He keeps himself informed about competitors' activities, particularly their successful or attempted take-overs of his own customers. He knows, too, which new prospects *he* has secured who previously were customers of theirs. In addition, he knows the main strengths and weaknesses of competitor products. He does not actively search for information about the novel, innovative, and creative moves of competitors in their early stages. He is satisfied to recognize them when they have become established trends. Thus he is not in a position to get a jump on his competitors but often is able to catch up after they have leapfrogged ahead of him.

A typical 5,5 sales attitude toward competitors is to "damn with faint praise." It is a way of appearing generous and statesmanlike while casting shadows that arouse doubt and uncertainty about the competitor. An alternative 5,5 attitude is the sliding yardstick approach of, "Theirs is good, but ours is better." In this way, criticism of the competitor is avoided, but in making the comparison, the sales-man has cleverly included praise of his own product. Another 5,5 approach is the sin of self-omission. This occurs when a weakness or deficiency in a competitor's product is pointed out, but the same weakness in the salesman's own product is ignored or played down. The strengths of the other product are denied by implication. The impact of this way of lessening the impact of competitors may be quite persuasive, especially when the customer is uninformed or has no means of checking on what the salesman says. But sowing the seeds of doubt is not a very effective way of being convincing, particu-larly when a prospect still remains unsold about the 5,5-oriented sales-man's product. He now has an added immunity provided by the skeptical attitude with which he has been inoculated.

The salesman's attitude toward knowledge, whether of product, customer, or competitor, is not that of intrinsic interest. His interest in knowledge is that it shields him from exposure to criticism by the customer.

PARTICIPATION AND INVOLVEMENT

The 5,5 attitude toward participation and involvement is influenced by his knowledge that the overpowering approach of 9,1 and the directionless socializing of 1,9 both have serious pitfalls. If he adopted either of these approaches, his customer would not view him as a really professional salesman. He does not want to be hardnosed or a "softy." He strives to balance his concern for making the sale with his concern for customer needs.

He is aware that his best chance to make a sale is to find out what the customer feels or thinks he needs. The salesman is expert in get-ting the customer to express these needs. He is alert to notice clues in what the customer is saying that may indicate particular tendencies, interests, and emotions that can be appealed to. Then he attempts to match his product to what the customer seems to want, or says he wants.[15] Every experienced salesman has had a customer whose ex-pressed needs were not the best expression of his actual needs. Other customers have wants that can be appealed to, but which presently are unrealistic for financial and other practical reasons.[16] Nevertheless, the 5,5-oriented salesman does not try to assist the customer in diagnosing the problem which would lead to the best decision for him. Instead, he has at his command a "cafeteria" of product applications which will meet the customer's expressed needs. He thus develops a skill in sounding out his man so that he can give him what he wants. This "cafeteria catalog" or line is likely to be remarkably similar to that of competitors, and price tends to be "what the traffic will bear."

The 5,5-oriented salesman probably has several clever but tricky sales techniques to get the customer to react positively and affirmatively. One way is to convert declarative statements into questions with which the prospect can be expected to agree. Question: That's a beautiful color, isn't it? Answer: Yes, it's pretty. Question: Nicely styled, isn't it? Answer: Yes, it is.

Figuratively hand in hand, down a path strewn with Yes-blossoms, the salesman attempts to lead his customer to the final purchase decision point. The proposition is made quite undramatically. It now seems just a matter of routine to answer Yes.[17]

Another variant of pseudo participation through questioning is the "cathedral chimes" technique. Again, the intention is to get the customer habituated to saying Yes. This time, however, he is assenting to attractive general propositions which are being made, between explanatory passages, in a series of sentences that ring the chimes through a number of evocative words. These suggest to the prospect that he is making a sound and personally rewarding decision. Note the harmonious chiming effect of, "Mr. Brown, do you *understand* how this service of ours is going to save you money? . . . Don't you *feel* your company would greatly *benefit* through insuring the safety of its work force? . . . Do you *appreciate* the freedom from worry that our service would give you and your employees? . . . Wouldn't you *like* to be out from under such a burden of responsibility as you are carrying at present?".

Another 5,5 way of trying to guide a customer through the use of participation is to give a boxed-in choice. Two alternatives are presented for the prospect's evaluation. But, whichever he comes to prefer, his option has been preplanned to be favorable to the salesman's end in making the sale.

Where a customer's needs cannot be matched either because of product or price, the 5,5 salesman will attempt to bring his customer to a compromise solution. The compromise is the most accepted decision-making process in the buy/sell relationship today. Participation and involvement is quite often dominated by attempts to reach compromise solutions on product usage, selling price, discounts, and so on.

Customer reactions to the 5,5 technique are unpredictable. Sometimes the salesman's strategy succeeds, particularly with customers who are in a hurry or for some reason are distracted and unable to concentrate fully on the criteria for making a sound purchasing decision. Nearly everyone can be swayed by subtle suggestions some of the time. But there is a strong likelihood also that any customer who encounters the salesman may be alert and aware, strongly committed to making the best use of his time and his own or his company's purchasing dollar. He only has to hear one false note in the salesman's presentation or comments and his suspicions are aroused. He watches and listens ever more keenly, and soon he begins to see through the surface film of illusion. The outline and movements of bait, line, and rod become apparent to him. If he does not instantly reject both the salesman and his product, the consequence will be that he begins acting in self-defense by thinking up objections that will put the salesman's smooth technique out of kilter.

Opening

A 5,5 attitude is that the gateway to a prospect's mind will surely open when he has been engaged in an initial conversation that builds up the salesman as a solid citizen and attractive personality, and so facilitates acceptance of his sales presentation. The opening phase may include a review of their acquaintances or a discussion of topics of general interest. This, hopefully, will bring salesman and customer to an early general unanimity out of which easy agreement on the sales transaction will emerge. The salesman is sizing up his customer and deciding what kinds of selling appeals he will use on him. If he cannot establish a climate of approval or if an attitude of customer disinterest is made evident, he moves quickly on through his other sales techniques that are geared to producing customer participation, whether genuine or not.

Sales Presentation

The sales presentation is also likely to be mechanical and routine, lacking the push of 9,1 and not attempting to evoke person-to-person emotional warmth as a 1,9 discussion might. Yet it is not passive in the sense of simply putting the product before the customer as occurs in 1,1 salesmanship. A 5,5 sales presentation is stereotyped. It follows a standard sequence with previously rehearsed points to be covered. These are presented in a way that lacks thoroughness and depth. They imply indirectly, rather than emphasize through flat statements, whatever merits the product possesses. The presentation is calculated to engage the prospect's interest and to occupy him in answering leading questions. The expected result is that he will have reviewed and assented to all the desirable qualities in the product. All of these will be in the forefront, for the question-and-answer process has made it difficult for him to concentrate on what might be the product's limitations or deficiencies. The motto is, "Accentuate the positive and eliminate the negative."

The salesman anticipates some of the risks of promoting customer hostility and seeks to avoid them. There is little direct pressuring and pushing. The salesman also can avoid the kind of transaction that would be "giving in to a customer." Thus, while he is not likely to press claims to justify an unreasonably high price, he is reluctant to make any adjustments in the buyer's favor that would shave sales margins. The 5,5 approach is not completely rigid or mechanical— there are flexibilities that the salesman can employ in responding to the situation. For instance, the salesman does not brush the customer's questions aside so as to continue his presentation. He has a repertoire of pat, rehearsed answers and is willing to give them on request. He will also respond to leads that are introduced by the customer's questions, and in this way can give closer attention to his needs, interests, and general situation. Because of a high reliance on the tried-and-true presentation, he is particularly vulnerable when vigorously probed by the customer. When his technique is punctured, he is likely to be unable to recoup because he has no ready response to cope with the unique situation. Under these circumstances he often tends to go 1,1.

Objections

The salesman operating under 5,5 assumptions is likely to adopt a compromising approach to customer objections. He has a capacity for living with contradictions rather than trying to solve them. He may suggest that an objection is partially justified, but not wholly so, and attempt to promote a positive attitude by indicating the better features of the product which compensate for any limitations that have been identified. If the customer raises two or more objections, the salesman may write these down on one side of a sheet of paper and then develop a longer list of reasons why the customer should buy. The suggestion, whether spoken or not, is that the customer's objections have been "outvoted." Or he may suggest that while the product might not meet all the customer's requirements, it does satisfy some essential ones. Another gambit is to try to sandwich the objection in between two positive features, pointing to a positive quality, acknowledging the limitation, but then moving on quickly to another positive quality. In this way the significance of the objection is reduced by the positive attributes with which the salesman surrounds the recognized limitation.

Another way of trying to meet an objection without dealing with it directly is through bargaining. It may involve a side deal—of throwing in a little "something extra"—to balance out the situation if the customer will accept the limitation and make a purchase.[18] This attitude of trying to compromise, bargain, and trade out with the customer to gain his acceptance of the product without meeting his objections directly is based upon a more general 5,5 disposition. It is to settle for what you can get rather than going after what is sound from the standpoint of solving the customer's problems in an objective way. The 5,5 motto is, "A half loaf is better than none."

Closing

The 5,5 sales technique in closing is part of the whole cloth along with the earlier parts of his presentation. He has a mental checklist of steps that he goes through in attempting to bring about a successful close. Many of its features are based upon gaining the customer's acceptance through suggestibility. These include appealing to his sense of pride in ownership or to his reputation in a company or in building his ego by suggesting that his status in the eyes of the community will be elevated as soon as his purchase becomes known. It has been suggested that many computers and executive jets have been sold with this as a significant basis for the decision.

If the formula does not produce results, the salesman is likely to become less tentative, pushing all the invisible "hot buttons" he sees that might induce the customer to buy. While still avoiding high-pressure techniques and without indulging in prophecies of doom, he will insert subtle remarks about what the customer runs the risk of losing if he makes a negative decision. If he still fails to close the sale and the customer is obviously about to break off the interview, he ventures some followup feelers. "Please let me contact you after you have had time to think about it." Or, "I'm disappointed because I've seen so many people benefit from this product. Perhaps I could introduce you to. . . ." Or, "I see that you are very busy so I won't take up any more of your time today. But I *would* like to stop by next week and discuss it some more."

ESTABLISHED BUSINESS

The 5,5-oriented salesman avoids taking established accounts for granted. He actively nurtures them without pressing hard. He often belongs to a "status" club where he can invite customers to meals or golf. He may have permanent seats in the local sports stadium. He often drives an expensive automobile.

Maintaining Accounts

One way of maintaining accounts is by making regularly scheduled visits to take the customer's pulse and to respond to whatever expanded sales opportunities there are. A second way is, through preparation, to try to focus the customer's attention on something different during each successive sales contact and to keep *him*—the customer—as the apparent focal point of the salesman's attention. These initiatives need have no direct connection with the product or service but may involve a tidbit of information, a suggestion about his vacation, a new way of thinking about his business situation, or any useful background fact the salesman may have learned from another customer, whose anonymity he will preserve. All of this is geared to feeding the customer by introducing fresh elements of interest. These contacts are more than "touching base." They are used to seek actively any further business from the customer, who comes to depend upon salesmen's eyes and ears for tidbits of gossip.

Complaints

He keeps alert for complaints, realizing that failure to deal with them can have an adverse effect on the steady, continuing business he desires. Often standard procedures have been worked out between him and his customer for dealing with the more common kinds of complaints. These may work well, keeping the customer's product satisfaction at a high level. In the absence of established procedures, a 5,5 way of dealing with a complaint is to reinterpret it in a different context so that, looked at from another way, it does not seem as important as it had previously appeared. When a complaint cannot be dealt with in either of these ways, another possibility is to try to adjust the difference. For example, if there were a commitment to deliver a thousand units and these units were held up by reasons of manufacturing difficulties, the salesman might try to find out from the customer the absolute minimum number needed to keep him going. The salesman would give a tentative promise to have this amount delivered quickly. Returning to his organization, he might double the customer's minimum order quantity and then permit himself to be bargained down by Production to the minimum number he had promised the customer. In this way an adjustment would be reached which would reduce the customer's frustration at having had no goods delivered. It would reduce the frustrations of the Production or Distribution people, because they would have beaten the Sales representative down from a large amount to a much smaller one for priority shipping. This is an all-round "workable" solution to a complaint, from the 5,5 angle. It does not solve the fundamental problem of why a promised delivery was not met, but it does bring the different points of view into an accommodation and adjustment which everyone can live with.

Rush Business

If his company can meet rush business without inconvenience, the 5,5-oriented salesman is more than pleased to take orders on this basis, emphasizing his readiness to give his customers special attention. If the company cannot easily adjust to rush business, his approach to the problem is similar to that illustrated in the previous section. It involves compromising and bargaining processes during which he seeks to move people toward an "equilibrium" level. This means that the customer would receive more than the Production or Distribution people initially indicated they could release but a lesser amount than the customer had at first considered essential. Through this kind of diplomacy, the customer's needs are at least partially met, yet the salesman avoids being charged with putting unreasonable demands on Production and Distribution. No one is entirely satisfied, but no one is left completely frustrated. Even more important, the risk of exposing this customer to aggressive selling of competitors is reduced, though of course not entirely eliminated.

INTEGRITY

A 5,5-oriented salesman does have respect for the truth. Yet he acts in such a way as to give himself a wide area of flexibility for seeking and then interpreting what the truth is. What is said is right, but what is left unsaid or what is implied leads to a conclusion that is not fully justified. He is very careful to toe the line on "what I actually said"— when all that was said *was* truth, but not *all truth* was said. A 5,5-oriented salesman confronted with a choice of making an invalid statement or remaining silent is quite conscious of "How things look on the record," "What's in the sales brochure," "What I don't dare get into," "Never say things you can't back up." All are 5,5 admonitions. His are most likely the "sins of omission." This is a "legalistic" concept of integrity. It ensures that the statements made will be true, while it provides a lot of leg room for leaving opportunities for the customer to draw unjustified implications and for the building of customer confidence which cannot be entirely realistic.

Subtle exaggerations are characteristic of him. He implies rather than says directly that the product will perform beyond its actual capabilities, especially if he has reason to believe that the customer is unlikely to utilize it at a rate approaching its capacity limits. Another way is to leave a misunderstanding uncorrected, particularly when a customer in his eagerness to have his needs fulfilled assumes that the product is more useful than it really is. When inevitably he is disillusioned, the salesman accepts no responsibility. In the most notorious instance he could say, "I have never claimed that it cures cancer." Otherwise, the usual regretful statement is, "I'm sorry, but it just didn't register with me that this was what you expected from our product."

Bluffing is a first cousin to the half-truth. It is where you commit yourself to doing something in the hope that you can deliver the goods. Having made the commitment, you try to live with it by taking the steps necessary for bringing about the result. This kind of a bluff is also found in 9,1. The difference is that a salesman exploiting the 9,1 bluff moves hell and high water to avoid having his bluff called. The 5,5 attitude is to have a bundle of excuses ready, and if these are unacceptable, to gain reacceptance through profuse apologies. The customer of a 1,9 salesman sometimes *feels* that he is being bluffed—the effect is the same—but the actual dynamic usually is that the salesman's undue optimism and his deep desire to please have trapped both of them unwittingly.

A customer's reaction to the 5,5 bluffing tactics is likely to be, "You have to take everything with a grain of salt." The customer comes to discount everything the salesman says and to look under the chip for the unspoken part of the statement.

SELF-MANAGEMENT

A 5,5-oriented salesman seeks the middle position. He neither wants to lead the pack nor to be out of step. He directs himself by taking what is typical of his colleagues inside himself as his own. His attitude is eclectic. If others find that a thing works, he uses it too, with but minor adjustments that make him feel that what he is doing is "his own thing." Routine and regularity aid him in feeling secure that he is doing what is expected of him.

Time   I schedule my activities well enough to achieve a good level of performance without pushing too hard. I ease the pressure on myself by adopting an orderly routine.

Prospecting   I follow through on most leads I get and create my own from lists and statistical documents. I increase my prospecting efforts whenever it appears I'm falling behind.

Servicing   I act as a go-between for the customer and my company's internal organization. A customer is entitled to fair treatment.

Expenses   I usually keep my expenses within the policy limits. At times, additional expenditures are required to capture sales opportunities.

Self-steering   Frequent self-appraisal helps me identify where I am out of step.[19]

The overall result from a 5,5-oriented salesman is likely to be that of maintaining present profitability levels. He works to keep a fair share of established accounts and to replace those lost with new business.

His attitude is, "Reasonable profit is built into our price structure and is necessary for company stability. Although I try to maintain price levels, I can't always keep customer goodwill and realize a profit at the same time."

It can be expected that a 5,5-oriented salesman will put the same degree of emphasis on profit as the company does and use price structure closely as his guide. However, he is likely to try to increase his sales volume by applying a "double standard" toward a price structure. For example, he may accept new business with a low profit margin, balancing it off against other business with a higher profit volume. In this way sales volume can be increased, profit levels kept constant, and total dollar saving increased. Thus he is likely only to introduce a slight degree of drag into the system when customer pressures are high.

CUSTOMER REACTIONS

The 5,5 selling approach is neither driving and fast in the 9,1 way nor drifting and slow in the 1,9 way. The salesman is most likely to pace his selling tempo to the customer's mood of the moment, moving along rapidly when the customer seems ready to go and slacking off when the customer is showing some doubt. In effect, the customer is the salesman's metronome.

What are the consequences of this 5,5 selling approach? Being stylized, it is not charged with high energy. It promotes illusions rather than arousing enthusiasm for what the product can really do. It does not genuinely involve the customer. The conviction and commitment it evokes in him may be strong enough to produce a sale, but being somewhat illusory, these tend to vanish afterward. The 5,5 approach can often be effective, particularly in moving highly reputable products when a customer finds himself in a situation where his desires for personal prestige are being appealed to or where for other reasons he feels a clear need for the product.

To a 9,1 customer, a 5,5 sales presentation has a hollow ring. It is unconvincing. The salesman's knowledge, as evidenced in the presentation or in reply to this customer's questions, is not sufficiently deep to give him full confidence that he is going to get his money's worth. His objections are parried and deflected rather than being dealt with by a slam-bang factual answer that would win his approval. The salesman's moderate energy and enthusiasm and the gimmicky aspects of his technique are not likely to move a 9,1 customer out of his dominant style. The salesman does not level with the customer in a way that would bring his responses more toward 9,9, and he is not convincing enough to pull a 9,1 customer into a complementary 5,5 attitude.

The 5,5 approach is more likely to be successful with a 1,9 customer, because there is much in it to please him and nothing to arouse his anxieties. For a 1,1 customer, however, most of the sales pitch is appealing to needs that do not exist for him. He is unlikely to be moved from his inertia.

A 5,5 customer may respond well to a 5,5 sales presentation. His questions are not so deep that they challenge the salesman's rather superficial knowledge. He will find nothing abrasive in the presentation, and the salesman moves at a tempo which is synchronized with his own.

A 9,9 customer usually finds the 5,5 presentation unconvincing, unless he comes to see—maybe without the salesman's aid—that this is a product or service which will fulfill his requirements. Otherwise this customer wants to hear more facts about the product, more logical connections between the facts to support the salesman's claims for the merits of his product, and more information about the relationship between the product's capabilities and the customer's objective needs. The customer brings enthusiasm and commitment to purchasing on this basis. His way of participating in the interview and the nature of his questions invite more openness and candor on the salesman's part, greater clarity in specifying what the product can and cannot do, its reliability in certain conditions in which it will be used, and so on. If the salesman responds to the customer's initiatives, he will in effect be shifting from his 5,5 dominant style into a 9,9 backup.

chapter eight

9,9

THE SALESMAN WITH a 9,9 predisposition places high value on reaching a sound sale-and-purchase decision with his customer. His main interest is in helping the customer make a reasoned purchase decision. This is to be a decision which the customer feels is right *and which has the highest probability, in the long run, of proving right.* The decision may, and probably is, reinforced by emotion at the time it is made. But during the discussion that leads up to it, the salesman is not attempting to overpersuade the customer with emotion-directed appeals so that he makes an unsound decision in the spirit of the moment. The salesman wants to work with the customer to find how a product or service can best contribute to satisfying the customer's needs or to resolve a problem that he has. This is "solution selling." The transaction must also be sound in terms of his company's objectives and marketing policies.

It is characteristic of the 9,9-oriented salesman that he listens for and seeks out ideas, opinions, and attitudes which differ from his own. The 9,9 focus is on the quality of thinking and its essential validity, regardless of whether it represents his own or a customer's view or emerges from their interaction. He is a real starter in the sense of initiating action, but he also follows through. Customers and others tend to pick up his sense of confidence in an enthusiastic way.

Whenever any conflict of ideas and emotions arises between the salesman and others, he tries to identify the reasons for it and resolve its underlying causes by working with the other person to gain insightful understanding of the facts and feelings that are involved. He rarely loses his temper, even when stirred up. His humor fits the situation. It is not used as a weapon or a lever or as oil to be poured on troubled waters; it helps to illuminate and clarify a situation. The more subjective elements of people's behavior—their feelings, attitudes, and fluctuating emotions—are recognized as essential ingredients of human experience and thus part of any sales interview. They cannot be kept out of it or kept separate during any part of it. They can facilitate good results as well as block them.

KNOWLEDGE: PRODUCT, CUSTOMER, AND COMPETITOR

An emphasis on fact-based solutions is one of the key features of a 9,9 selling orientation. Product, customer, and competitor facts are data to be considered together.

Recognizing the persuasive power of knowledge, a 9,9-oriented salesman builds self-reliance by acquiring expert knowledge of his product. He does this through continuous study, analysis, and inquiry about the qualities of the product itself. He takes every opportunity to consult with the technical specialists who design and manufacture the product he is selling. He keeps himself well informed of his established customers' experiences in using the product. As a result, he has little need to rely on others to support the knowledge he has gained. On the occasions when he does refer to others for special product advice, his needs for information usually relate to new innovative applications which involve technical understanding beyond what could be expected of a person whose primary job is selling.

Since, by his definition, customers are people who have problems for which his product may provide solutions, the salesman makes sure that he knows and understands each customer's situation. He seeks to apply his product knowledge *after* finding out how the product might benefit the customer he is interviewing. In the process, he becomes informed of whatever alternative products and services the prospect has considered or experimented with. He also comes to know more about the customer himself.

The emotions of a customer, as well as the customer's objective situation, *are facts to the salesman.* The capacity to respond to a customer's interests, desires, and aspirations is an attribute of the salesman's knowledge about him. The way in which a salesman responds reflects the quality of his concern for the customer. Many apparent "shortcuts" are ethically unsound, and counterproductive in terms of results. To encourage a speedy purchase decision by appealing to feelings and aspirations which a salesman knows will not be satisfied by his product is only to create a likelihood that the customer's expectations will be violated after such a purchase. In these circumstances the salesman's loss—in terms of future business—may be more than in proportion to the customer's disappointment. Disgruntled purchasers "counteradvertise" products and salesmen.

A 9,9-oriented salesman is unlikely to bring on these consequences. He actively works to eliminate them as possibilities. His high concern both for the customer and for the quality of the sales result leads him to check and make sure that the customer's expectations of what he will gain by purchasing are completely realistic. In preparation, he must first get to know the needs and problems that will influence the customer's expectations as he considers what he sees and is told about the product.

In pursuing these unified concerns, the 9,9-oriented salesman may frequently come to understand the customer's problems more clearly than the customer himself, who is deeply embedded in his own circumstances and may not be seeing them as objectively as an outside observer—the salesman—can. Thus, the interview evolves as a situation in which two people are deliberating together about how one of them can best use the product and what the best choice between alternatives is, rather than Person A pressing the product upon Person B.

The 9,9-oriented salesman realizes that his company's competitors are offering solutions to customers' problems, too. So as to be able to compete successfully, he needs to aim at understanding *their* products as thoroughly and comprehensively as he does his own. In reading and through trade contacts, he seeks out what experiences other consumers are having with competitor products. This is in parallel with the way he keeps himself informed of his own established customers' experiences with his product. He may experiment by using the competitive product himself or by dismantling, examining, and reassembling it so as to understand its manufacturing and operational characteristics. His company may take responsibility for analyzing the more expensive and complex competitor products and then circulating useful information to its salesmen. The benefit from gaining this kind of knowledge is that it enables the 9,9-oriented salesman to reply factually and analytically to customer inquiries at a time when the customer is trying to get an idea of how his product compares with the competitor's.

Often a customer will begin to think comparatively about "this product versus the other product" during a sales interview. He may feel that he does not have enough data to make a good evaluation of both products. At the moment, the salesman is the only source of information he can draw from. He decides to ask, even though he is skeptical about how objective an answer he will receive. So in effect, the customer is applying a test to the salesman. If he detects a substantial bias against a competitor's product, he may well infer a correspondingly unfactual slant in the other direction, in whatever the salesman is saying about his own product.

As we have seen, a salesman with a 9,9 attitude is likely to be better informed about competitors' strategies, pricing, and product characteristics than the 9,1-oriented salesman who also takes a keen interest in competitors. The major difference is that the 9,9-oriented person has informed himself in an objective way. He views his competitor with respect and is ready to run a fair race with him, confident of his own product's ability to lead the field. If a customer wants to talk about competitors' products in relation to his own, he is prepared to comment objectively on the relative merits of each. His own comments or conclusions are supported by facts, performance data, and logic. This is by no means to say that the salesman adopts the attitude of a scientist making a cold comparison. In presenting his views in this way, he is acknowledging that the prospect *is* going to make comparisons, either during this interview or at some other time before making up his mind, and that these comparisons will be pivotal in the decision whether or not to purchase his product. Putting himself in the prospect's shoes, he is in an excellent position to set up the kind of comparative framework that the customer can use. While doing this, he can demonstrate the unique advantages of his own product without tearing down his competitor. This kind of open-minded objectivity lays a good foundation for building the prospect's confidence in the salesman and his products rather than in a competitor's.

Why is so much emphasis placed on comparison of one's own products with those of a competitor? The answer is apparent when you step into the customer's shoes for a moment. The customer's needs are best served when he can make a choice from a variety of products presented by several different salesmen. This range permits him to compare and choose and make his final selection from a range of comparable products, a spectrum of prices, and an array of servicing provisions. The mental attitude of a salesman, whose interests are served by the customer purchasing his product, is understandably different from the mental attitude of his customer. But the salesman should not consider his own attitude to be the rule of life. If the salesman unwittingly assumes that the customer knows his product as well as he knows it himself, that the customer *should* be eager to select his product and disregard the competitor's, that the customer is unconcerned about the relative prices of competitive products, or that he is not comparing his own servicing arrangements with those offered by competitors, he is living in a world of hope, not of reality. Consequently, he is less likely to be effective during the interview and in bringing about a close than if he had been continually alert to the differences between his own "natural" mental attitude and that of the customer.

The primitive, unreasoned inclination of a salesman, then, is to reduce a customer's opportunities for comparing the products which the salesman handles with those of competitors. The natural inclination of a customer is to try to increase the possibilities of comparison. Some salesmen want to restrict comparison in order to avoid the negative results—in terms of fewer sales—that the customer's wide-ranging consideration of competitors' products might lead to. The customer wants to increase his comparison opportunities in order to have a stronger basis on which to found his purchasing decision.

The 9,9 sales approach does not rest on the assumption that it is necessary to keep a set of blinders on the customer to induce him to accept your product in preference to a competitor's. Instead, the assumption is that when a salesman can assist his customer to compare products in a sound and valid way, he is in a stronger position to gain the customer's confidence and respect. He is also in a better position to forward his own product against the background of "silent comparisons" which the customer is probably making whether the salesman realizes it or not.

Is this to be interpreted as meaning that people are mostly "fact, data, and logic" oriented, and rarely make purchasing decisions that are influenced by status considerations or emotions or other subjective factors? The answer is No. Many purchasing decisions are weighted with heavy status and prestige rationales which are more subjective and emotional than factual and reasoned. In the final analysis, perhaps most purchasing decisions are triggered by an emotional feeling of, "This is what I want."

The point is this. Decisions that are based on fact and reason are likely to be more durable and rewarding than those that are based solely on impulse and emotion. Over the long term, they are likely to provide continued satisfaction as the product is used and its suitability is confirmed. There is less disappointment as the first glow of ownership recedes. A 9,9-oriented salesman would be reluctant to make a snap close of the sale, based solely on a customer's speedily heightened emotions and impulse to buy. He prefers to keep the decision open a while longer so that the light of data and logic can shine on it. Often he finds that the added intellectual appreciation reinforces his customer's emotional desires. The result is a stronger sale and an increased likelihood of a steady and improving account. Had the purchase been made merely on a basis of unreasoned enthusiasm, without the customer's having a good appreciation of how the product could precisely fit his needs and wishes, he might easily have become disillusioned with it later on and blamed the salesman. Thus, being able to combine deep product knowledge with a sound understanding of the prospect's situation, the 9,9-oriented salesman is uniquely capable of forwarding his own product in a positive and constructive way.

The attitude of openness and candor that typifies a 9,9 sales orienta-tion, as described here, can result in a lost sale if it becomes obvious to salesman and customer alike that a competitor's product is an obviously better answer to his needs. Does this mean that a 9,9 sales orientation is harmful to his company's interests? No, it means the opposite. If his product is not competitive with another one for satisfying a par-ticular category of customer needs, he and his company know it. They are alerted to the situation and can take any necessary steps to improve their competitiveness in that area.[20]

PARTICIPATION AND INVOLVEMENT

The key to the 9,9 approach to selling is integrating two concerns. One is a genuine concern on the part of the salesman for creating sound, profitable, and continuing business for his company. The other is for ensuring that the customer makes the kind of purchase that is most closely attuned to his requirements. There is no contradiction between these two concerns; they unite, providing a unified and authentic professional approach.

9,9 is *the* participation and involvement selling approach. The closing is reached only when there is a genuine mind-meeting con-sensus. The understanding and agreement between salesman and cus-tomer are reinforced by feelings of emotional validity—that the pur-chase decision is right.

How can this kind of understanding between customer and sales-man come about? The salesman sets the pace from his general atti-tudes and his approach to creating a climate of give and take. He does this by exploring with the customer what his actual requirements are and how best these can be satisfied within the usual limits that need to be acknowledged by both parties. These are the unmodifiable (in the short run) features of the product or services on the one hand and any financial or budgetary limitations the customer may have on the other. Within these boundaries is an area where a sound sale-and-purchase transaction may be reached, satisfactory from the point of view of each party. This is not to say that the salesman enters the interview with the fixed conviction that his product or service will inevitably satisfy the customer's needs. He thinks this is possible and likely. His involvement lies in selling to the customer in a way that most fully satisfies his realistic requirements. However, it might become evident, as the customer's requirements and the product's applicability are brought out and compared, that the product cannot be fitted to the customer's needs or financial capability. In these circumstances, the salesman will voluntarily point this out and give whatever helpful advice he can so as not to leave the customer stranded.

The 9,9-oriented salesman comes to his customer bringing objective facts and data on his product, combined with a responsible attitude toward using them. In addition, he is prepared to contribute any and all imaginative powers that he possesses. He will probably not present all his facts at the beginning of the interview. Product facts, by themselves, are not useful until they can be related to a customer's requirements. Neither would he withhold any facts as the interview proceeds. The customer has full access to his "data bank." Many times the effective communication of understanding can be moved from abstract to concrete levels by selling aids which can provide pictures, examples of use, graphs, and charts that support straightforward conclusions from an otherwise complex array of statistics, and so on.

The salesman needs to have information from the customer concerning his situation and requirements, and so will seek his active participation from the outset. Soon it is likely that they will be working together in a give-and-take discussion to locate the area in which genuine customer-salesman consensus can be found. The salesman has a keen commitment to participation and involvement with his customer. The latter, whatever his initial reservations, notices this and responds to it with growing participation and involvement in the interview. The consequences of this trend are that he becomes both intellectually and emotionally involved in making a sound purchase. In this way, the consensus which is reached between salesman and customer is on a basis of genuine partnership in arriving at a mutually beneficial transaction. It begins a selling-purchasing relationship but is likely to endure and to generate future business.

Opening

The 9,9 strategy is one of gaining access to the customer's mind. The salesman might open by inquiring of the customer whether he is currently acquainted with the product, if he has had any experience with it, or if he knows others who have. The salesman wants to sample and test the customer's knowledge first, so as to correct it if there is misunderstanding and so as not to become repetitious when he makes his presentation. From this kind of opening, the customer is likely to feel that his time will be well used. He will be given all additional data he needs and will be placed in a situation where he can make a sound business judgment rather than buy something that he fully understands only after ownership has been transferred.

If the customer appears indifferent or reserved during this initial exploratory period, the 9,9-oriented salesman seeks to understand what the barriers to establishing a mutually advantageous business relationship are. He might say, "After I've had the opportunity to present the facts, if you do continue to be uninterested, at least we will both know that it's a disinterest founded on logic and understanding. This is something that I can appreciate, but I would like to have an opportunity to establish what these reservations are, rather than simply to assume that we can't really provide you with a useful product or service." In responding to this kind of inquiry, the prospect is likely to be stimulated to run a mental check on his current situation. The salesman has not only stated his motive; he is giving the customer an opportunity to pursue and, hopefully, to satisfy his own business or personal interests in the discussion that follows. It begins to be apparent to the customer that this salesman is not trying to gain personal dominance over him, nor is he coaxing or indirect in his approach. What the salesman has to say is purposeful yet authentic. He has set the keynote of frankness for a productive discussion.

Now that the salesman has gauged the customer's knowledge and dealt with any initial reservations, the interview can develop into a more detailed examination of the product and how it may contribute to solving one or more of the customer's problems. The salesman can now go on to build up the customer's knowledge and understanding of his product and to deal with the essential issues. These will be taken according to their relative importance in helping the customer to relate product facts to his own situation and so reach his decision.

Sales Interview

A 9,9 sales interview is of quite a different character than any of those that have previously been discussed. There are several assumptions on which it is based. One is that the sales presentation is not a pitch, but an interview. Another is that the salesman should previously have become clear about the customer's needs for his product as the basis for organizing his presentation. A third is that facts, data, logic, and evidence are the soundest bases for bringing about a positive decision to purchase. The fourth is that customers are acknowledged to be thinking people who are entitled to be treated with respect.

Given these kinds of assumptions, what is a 9,9 sales interview like? If the salesman found that the customer was not well informed about his product during the opening, he might begin by spelling out in a general way the benefits that the customer could reasonably expect to receive from the product if he purchased it. He goes on to aid the customer in defining and specifying his needs and his particular problems in the area served by the product. This is a significant factor in promoting his interest. The salesman can then continue to describe the product in a way that correlates its functions with the customer requirements that it can satisfy. As the interview proceeds, he listens and questions so as to extend his knowledge of the customer's situation and thus gain deeper understanding of how his product might provide the greatest benefit to this customer.

The 9,9-oriented salesman is a realist. His product knowledge tells him where the outer boundaries of the product's usefulness are situated, and he recognizes them. He tries to anticipate possible misunderstandings and to correct these as he goes along, probing to ensure that the customer is with him. He is committed to creating realistic expectations on the customer's part concerning what the product will or will not do for him if he purchases it.

This kind of selling is a two-way street. It has flexibility in the sense that the interview "fits" the needs and requirements of the customer. This is achieved as the salesman actively involves the customer in the interview and helps him develop his understanding of what the product can do specifically for him. As the customer comes to see for himself that the product answers his requirements, his enthusiasm and conviction amass into a purchasing decision.

Acting on 9,9 assumptions, the salesman begins bringing his customer into participation and involvement at the same time he is introducing the product. The presentation is not in the flat lecturer-to-audience form that many salesmen imply under their faulty "description first, persuasion later" assumptions. There are many ways in which this can be done. One is for the salesman to ask the customer appropriate questions, not of a temperature-taking variety, but questions that stimulate the customer to get the salesman involved in *his*— the customer's—situation. The salesman is as ready and eager to develop a firsthand understanding of the customer's situation as he is for the customer to build direct experience with the product. This salesman is willing to probe, to analyze, to put himself into situations. As the collaboration grows, he will actively experiment along with the customer to see how the product fits the conditions in which it is to be used. This is far more than a desk-level demonstration. It is a demonstration by experiment in a situation of use. Here the salesman is qualified by his unified knowledge of product and customer to speak convincingly of how the product can function to provide a solution to his problem.

There are other natural and positive ways in which participation and involvement can be linked together. One means is to enable a prospect to see, hear, touch, feel, handle, try on, test the product for size, or interact with it in other ways. As he does so, the 9,9-oriented salesman introduces thoughts and ideas which help the prospect to understand and join reason to his feelings as they develop. As both his understandings of the product itself and of the feelings he is experiencing increase, he is building for himself a rational basis for respecting the product. He can consider his requirements on the factual and rational plane and find that the product meets them. His emotions support this understanding. His liking for the product has grown simultaneously with his understanding of it. He is fully and naturally committed. His evaluation is not tinged with skepticism that he might have been led too far by rhetoric and pressure. The salesman has aided the customer's understanding, and the customer has convinced himself that he needs the product. He is ready to purchase in order to have it.

Some products are of the kind that do not lend themselves to direct tryout and experience by the customer during the sales interview. For example, the product may be a machine that can only be delivered and installed in the future. It can be a long-term service that is not realistically "sampled" during the interview. There are ways of arranging for the customer to participate and involve himself with it other than to "have been there himself." If at first he cannot visualize himself using it, the salesman can describe how he could do so and what the advantages would be. Examples can be drawn from the experiences of others who own the product or make use of it. The salesman does not refer to them in a name-dropping way to suggest the prestige of his product. The description of how others use the product is intended to aid the customer in experiencing their thinking and emotions to some extent, thereby coming to know more intimately what the product is like. Where possible, the salesman will arrange visits to users and be with the customer during these visits. While the customer is seeing and hearing how others utilize the product or service, new ideas are being introduced which can fire up his personal involvement.

Objections

The kind of participation and involvement that is so central to establishing the creative interplay between thoughts and emotions comes to the forefront in the area of "objections." The 9,9-oriented salesman's attitude toward objections is one of the most significant of his attributes which lead to a valid sale and a satisfied customer.

Almost invariably the customer has doubts and other reservations as he views the product for the first time. The salesman recognizes this fact. He creates opportunities for the customer to express and discuss his misgivings early in the interview. He knows that if these are not brought out, they probably will persist, unmodified, to influence the customer's thinking and feeling throughout the interview. If he can get them expressed openly, then he has an opportunity to remove them as barriers to purchasing.

There are several kinds of reservations. Some are because of lack of information about the product. Initially, the customer may be hesitant to reveal his objections. He wants to get an idea of the kind of man he is dealing with before he opens up. If he feels that the salesman is one who suppresses disagreement or rebuts it with specious arguments, he is likely to sit on his objections and look for an opportunity to terminate the interview. However, the 9,9-oriented salesman shows in his manner as well as by a spoken invitation that he welcomes a customer's queries and comments, whether favorable or not. He listens so as to understand the customer's views. He may ask supplementary questions, not in an attacking way but to find where the customer's product knowledge needs to be strengthened. Only then will he be in a position to provide the necessary information to the customer so as to dissolve his initial objection and gain his support of the product.

Other objections may be based on misinformation about the functions, quality, usefulness, and other attributes of the product. The salesman who invites his customer into real participation with him in examining the product creates opportunities to find out what these misunderstandings actually are. The salesman can then replace the misinformation with valid information that removes this kind of objection.

Sometimes a customer's unstated objections are founded upon reservations and doubts which are rooted solely in the customer's feelings. The customer may be quite unaware that emotions are affecting his objectivity. By inviting the customer to say whatever he feels about the product and then listening attentively, the salesman may come to understand what is bothering him. As an example, his product may be the current scapegoat of a customer's strong general prejudice against a whole category of items. For instance, the customer may object to a chemical product or treatment because he considers it "artificial." Even in as difficult a case as this, a customer's initial reactions can be replaced with the enthusiasm of emotional involvement if the salesman first finds out what the product's objectionable features are, as viewed through the customer's distorting lens. When a salesman can deal with illogical and emotion-based reactions calmly, providing facts within structures of thinking that help the customer to gain better insights into what the product can do for him, he has a chance to free himself from these emotional shackles. If the salesman is genuinely trying to bring out the customer's reservations and objections for discussion—rather than as ammunition to win arguments and put him down—the customer will usually recognize his honest motive and respect him for it. Generally, people do respond to authentic feelings of concern to understand their points of view. This in turn often helps them to respond to alternatives when these are presented.

When a customer's objection is based on genuine and valid points, the 9,9 way is to acknowledge the objection, then openly explore realistic possibilities for dealing conclusively with it. This may involve probing in order to get to the root of the customer's thinking. More often than not, when an objection or disagreement is discussed openly and with candor, one of two things happens. It either turns out to have been less important than it first appeared, or creative ways can be found for having the product or service made to correspond more fully with the customer's needs.

This way of openly confronting conflict can promote true understanding and respect between salesman and customer. It provides the best method of finding a sound basis of resolution to any point of disagreement. It involves emotions and feelings in a constructive way, removing those that are barriers and replacing them with enthusiastic convictions and commitment. It avoids selling a customer in a way that would result in his having his expectations violated and crushed later on. Of course, a longer time has to be taken to reach a 9,9 consensus than it might take a 9,1-oriented salesman to overwhelm and crush an objection. However, the 9,9 approach is time-conserving over the long haul. It does permit men to disagree and then to resolve their disagreements after searching out the right facts, data, and reasoning needed to reach a true meeting of minds. It is a problem-solving approach where the salesman is as committed to the customer's needs being fulfilled as the customer is interested in making a sound purchase.

Closing

The 9,9 closing contains a number of distinctive features. One of these is summing up. This is not the loaded machine-gun summary of benefits that a 9,1-oriented salesman sometimes employs, nor is it a bald statement of "pros and cons" which leaves the customer feeling that the interview has been inconclusive and that he should consult someone else before making up his mind. The 9,9 summing up helps the customer to crystallize his thinking and weigh his decision in the light of all the major points previously developed. In this manner the salesman helps his customer in reaching a positive decision, because this decision can be considered, confirmed, and made in an integrated context, not just on the last few issues that have been discussed. These may be the most vivid ones in his memory but might not be seen in good perspective with the rest.

Another feature is in checking through with the customer all points that have been made in the summing up to ensure that these are understood, while at the same time the customer is invited to pose additional inquiries, if he has any. This is not asking the customer to think up and express new reservations and doubts. It provides him with the opportunity to identify ones that may not yet have been expressed—ones which have not become evident to the salesman although the customer is still wrestling with them. Finally, a 9,9-oriented salesman can be expected to express his own convictions and enthusiasm about the benefits that the customer can look forward to when making a positive decision.

If a positive decision is not reached at this point, the salesman does not increase his pressure to close, but instead shows a strong interest in understanding the customer's reasons. This is not for the purpose of knocking them down, although any newly identified misunderstandings can be dealt with. The likelihood of converting a negative to a positive decision is still at hand. But mainly the salesman's interest is for a deeper reason: to gain a fuller understanding of what barriers are blocking the customer's positive decision. This can aid him in anticipating similar problems with future customers. It may yield valuable information for him to transmit back to his organization so that some real problems—the product's functional limitations, its quality and pricing in relation to competitors', and so on—can be dealt with and solved.[21] Finally, this kind of debriefing provides a good basis for a later return call that could make a difference, for example, when the prospect's situation changes or when the salesman has a different product or terms on which to negotiate.

The 9,9 way of closing yields the maximum possibility of bringing about a successful sales result. It is not so pressure-based as to polarize a customer into a negative attitude. It is not so yielding to the customer's attitude as to lose his confidence. It is not so matter-of-fact as to fail to stimulate his enthusiasm, nor is it so pat as to tarnish his desire. Rather, being based upon factual information which is unified by logic and is enthusiasm-generating through involvement and participation, it is most likely to lead the customer to a positive commitment.

ESTABLISHED BUSINESS

When the kind of sales interview that we have just described has been brought to a successful closing, an excellent foundation has been laid for repeat orders and expanding business from this customer. The 9,9 knowledge-based and problem-solving orientations, unlike some other salesmen styles, do not impact on a customer in ways that make him resistant to future sales. On the contrary, the customer is likely to summon the salesman whenever he confronts a problem which the salesman can help him think through and solve.

Maintaining Accounts

A 9,9-oriented salesman can be expected to do several other things to maintain established business. One is to keep in touch with the customer on a regular schedule. The frequency of visiting is determined by analyzing the customer's situation and estimating when he is likely to be ready to place new orders. He also follows up to seek out any dissatisfactions or reservations that the customer may feel but is not yet raising to the level of a "complaint." In this way he can spot difficulties that may lie silent yet would harm the possibility that repeat business will come his way. Another way of maintaining accounts is to arrange special contacts and visits whenever he learns of new developments on the customer's side and whenever there are changes in his company's products about which the customer needs to know. In maintaining the relationship in these ways, he reduces the risk of the customer's being taken over by competitors and increases the possibility of expanding business with his established accounts.

Complaints

Complaints are a warning signal to the 9,9-oriented salesman. Unless he knows what they are and deals with them promptly and effectively, they can grow into widespread customer discontent. He is prepared to take action immediately. No matter how small the complaint may appear in his eyes, he realizes that it is not small in the eyes of the customer.

The salesman gets with his customer as quickly as possible. He encourages him to lay out the full story, with all details of the product's role in it, and to express his feelings from the standpoint of what he thinks should have been done by the company but was not. Where the product's or the company's performance is at fault, the salesman frankly acknowledges this failure. He makes it clear that he appreciates the customer's openness. Using his product knowledge but staying within the limits of his technical ability, he outlines the surest way of righting the situation he can find, checks it out with the technical specialists in his company, and reaches agreement with the customer on what is to be done. He follows up to ensure that the needed actions result.

Rush Business

Rush business is both an opportunity and a hazard. It is an opportunity to increase sales volume. The hazard that it contains is twofold. One aspect is that when a customer's desires cannot be met, his door is open to competitors who may be able to satisfy his needs. The other is that while it may be possible to fulfill rush orders, the expense of doing so may make the effort unprofitable.

Thus the 9,9-oriented salesman probes to understand what are the reasons for the rush, to see if there is another way to handle the situation. If not, he discusses the problem with Manufacturing or Distribution to see how it can be handled. Sometimes a rescheduling of deliveries can be arranged without causing inconvenience to other customers of the company, but frequently this is impractical. In any case, the salesman stays with the problem until the customer is satisfied. This may mean going out to find an emergency source of supply at no profit to himself. Finally, he sits down with the customer to help him think through his future requirements in order to anticipate his needs and so avoid further rush orders as far as possible.

INTEGRITY

Integrity is found in the 9,9 orientation. Truth is sought through openness, candor, and in acknowledging limitations.

Whereas the 9,1 attitude is based on the idea that an invalid means may be justified by a valid end, that is, by making a sale, the 9,9 attitude is that valid ends have the great likelihood of being reached when valid means are employed to approach them.

The information exchanged between salesman and customer leads to realistic and valid expectations. It is straight shooting. There is no hesitation on the salesman's part, for example, to promise delivery. But he will estimate and state clearly, on a realistic basis, how much certainty or uncertainty there is that delivery will be possible on the target date. Where statements cannot be made objectively but involve interpretation and judgments, the 9,9-oriented salesman feels no reluctance about giving his views. But he always gives notice to his listener when a statement is factually based and when his own interpretations and judgments are being introduced. In this way he may forward statements that are not factually certain. Nevertheless he has let the customer know the components of fact and opinion within the statement. Thus the customer has a basis for weighing the predictability of the statement in his own mind and applying whatever alternative interpretations he prefers.

Another aspect of 9,9 integrity is in the salesman's ability to say, "I don't know." It's been mentioned that the 1,1 salesman says this sometimes. What, then, is the difference between the 1,1 statement, "I don't know," and the 9,9 kind? The 1,1 "I don't know" might be said when, in fact, he does know, and this is likely to be often. Or it may be a frank admission that he doesn't know, with the unspoken supplement, ". . . and I couldn't care less." The 9,9 "I don't know" is also a frank admission, which has the spoken addition, ". . . but I'll find out." A 9,9 "I don't know" is always acceptable and can be counted upon to increase respect because it occurs in the context of other 9,9 attributes. Product knowledge and customer knowledge are the basis of the salesman's demonstrated competence. The customer can accept the occasional "I don't know" and say to himself, "There is an open man. In this kind of situation, even when I might never have detected his lack of information, he readily admits it and puts a binding commitment on himself to remedy it so that I can know what I'm going into. What a contrast to the other salesmen who just go on aggressively pushing, or who seem to float on a cloud of wishful thinking, or who cover their ignorance by implying that the question's not important!"

SELF-MANAGEMENT

Self-management is an apt description of the 9,9-oriented salesman. He has the skills of setting personal selling objectives and applying his energy in result-oriented ways. Thus, he is autonomous. Because his orientation is a problem-solving one, he is not only able to maintain self-direction but also is alert to changes in situations that call for shifts in direction.

He is best pictured as having an experimental attitude, continually searching for ways to strengthen strategies that work well and to discover new ones by trying to solve the unknown or what is not understood in each selling situation. He uses feedback from customers, both in the ongoing selling situation and in a later critique of his efforts, to aid him to learn from the experiences he has regarding strong and weak features in his presentation and approach.

Time I put effort into scheduling my activities in terms of sales objectives. In this way it is possible to perform all my responsibilities, and emergencies are rare.

Prospecting Prospecting is vital to sales growth. I see every customer as a gatekeeper who can open the door for new business. Existing customers are analyzed for the categories they represent with effort concentrated on new contacts in the most favorable categories first.

Servicing I see that my commitments are met and top service is provided. By following through with the customer, I try to anticipate his servicing requirements. The customer has paid for sound treatment, and his continued satisfaction increases the strength of the account.

Expenses The expenses put under my control are essential in doing business, and my integrity and prudence provide guidance as I incur them. Full value in terms of sales results should be realized from the money I spend.

Self-steering I improve my skills and increase my professional contribution by analyzing reasons for failures as well as successes.[22]

The 9,9-oriented salesman keeps in perspective the complex and subtle factors that enter into ensuring that a sale is profitable. He does not automatically assume that nothing must stand in the way of an order, as is likely to be true for a 9,1 approach, or that nothing is too much for a customer, as a 1,9 orientation might suggest. Rather, his attitude is, "Business is conducted for making a profit. When there is any question of not putting primary emphasis on the profitability of a transaction, all related factors must be considered. My objective is profitable selling with full customer satisfaction. This is in the best long-term interest of my company, my customers, and myself."

He is constantly striving to upgrade the product his accounts are purchasing as well as to maintain the profit margins on his sales. In this way sales volume can be increased, dollar volume of earnings improved, and profitability heightened.

Many products of today are so complex that it has become impossible for a single salesman to represent them in a comprehensive way. This is particularly so when the customer solutions involve systems concepts, such as in advanced process control,[23] traffic and transportation, and in defense-supply industry contexts. Similar considerations apply when a company manufactures a number of different specialized products, many of which could be marketed to some very large potential customers.[24] The difficulty here is that any individual salesman's deep knowledge is limited to one or a few products or elements of the total system. Conversely, a very large company's purchasing agents and the potential users of the products or system may be specialists as well. In view of the possible size of the total sale, both supplier and customer companies may find it most convenient to negotiate an overall purchasing contract or set of contracts. This is done after the whole range of products or the entire system has been presented by a team of specialist salesmen and considered by a team of specialist purchasing agents.

This kind of situation calls for *teamwork*. It entails cooperative effort by two or more salesmen who, together and jointly but not separately and individually, possess the full capability for representing the total product. On the purchasing side too, integrated knowledge and a coordinated approach are essential.[25] Aside from benefits obtained from comprehensive and large-scale selling and purchasing, much useful operational knowledge can be shared and new insights gained.[26] 9,9 properties of team selling are not further discussed here, since the character of teamwork, and of teams in interaction, is more fully analyzed in detail elsewhere.[27]

All things considered then, it does appear that a 9,9 salesman orientation confronts the fewest risks to profitable selling, particularly when viewed in a long-term perspective. It probably brings the greatest possible benefits of expanded sales volume and customer satisfaction from both new and established accounts.

CUSTOMER REACTIONS

A 9,9 sales orientation has the greatest likelihood of achieving positive consequences. This is so with customers of any Grid style. There is a simple reason for this. The 9,9 assumptions provide a valid basis for getting a fit between the salesman's products and the customer's wants. Having a high concern for the customer's problem, it appeals to the 9,1 customer's objective of making a good purchase, although he is likely to find that this salesman cannot be pressured into unjustifiable concessions. He will sense that the salesman possesses energies and commitment that match his own but are directed toward exploring with him the usefulness of the product in relation to his needs. Being open and aboveboard, the 9,9 approach does not arouse his suspiciousness, or if this is already present, it may reduce his fears of being taken.

Because it is predicated on understanding the customer's situation and has a high concern for a customer, a 9,9 sales approach meets the 1,9 customer's desire to be liked. His respect for the salesman is increased by his involvement in a sound purchase. Thus the 9,9-oriented salesman can readily bring a 1,9 customer into agreement.

His approach has the likelihood of being able to activate a backup style in the 1,1 customer, stimulating an interest which would other wise lie dormant.

The same is true for a 5,5 customer. It converts his customary reliance on the traditional and time-tested into a greater readiness to consider innovative and creative possibilities. However novel and nonconventional the product, when the customer can see how it fits his needs, the former tentativeness can change to a confident purchase decision.

With a 9,9 customer, the approach clicks immediately, because the interview is geared not only to responding to his needs but also to doing so based on fact, data, and logical reasoning, with efforts to ensure that his expectations about the product are realistic and valid.

What are the implications of adopting a 9,9 orientation toward every customer contacted? Does this kind of solution selling restrict a salesman, extinguishing his spontaneity and stereotyping his behavior? Is this salesman an idealistic "saint with a sample case?" No—9,9 opens new doors into becoming more flexible, creative, and individual-centered in one's sales approach.

Why? Solution selling within the 9,9 orientation gives a salesman his greatest flexibility. Because he thinks in problem-solving terms, he is more likely to get on the same wavelength as the customer and to do so quickly.

Formulating issues in terms of alternatives and options, and weighing the pros and cons of each, increases the likelihood that a "best-fit" solution will be found. Gearing his presentation to facts, data, and logic promotes more realistic expectations of what consequences the purchase decision will have. Conducting his interview as a two-person participation and involvement situation increases the probability that the consistent appeal to the customer's logic and profoundest self-interest will resonate with his emotions and feelings.

All of this generates a customer's respect for him and appreciation of his competence. The result is that customer confidence is heightened and that any doubts which might lead to reluctance to purchase are reduced. The greatest flexibility, then, comes from a 9,9 solution-selling orientation which opens up more situational variables to examination, produces a deeper, more valid human contact between salesman and customer, and gears a sales presentation to need-fulfilling performance rather than the creation of hopeful illusions that would later be followed by disillusion.

Another aspect of how to increase the possibility of 9,9 problem solving between salesman and customer can now be pointed out. It has been repeatedly observed that most customers have a wide range and variety of Grid style attitudes that can influence their personal behavior in different situations. This means that almost anyone can operate under a 9,9 problem-solving orientation should the right circumstances be created. Thus, the conclusion is that a salesman should try to maintain a 9,9 sales orientation which, other things being equal, is most likely to produce a good sales result. If he does this, he stands a good chance of being able to lead his customer into adopting the same orientation while responding to the salesman. Then their two attitudes complement each other to the advantage and benefit of both. The salesman has the greatest likelihood of effecting a sale and the customer has the greatest likelihood of making a purchase when the action of each is based upon convictions which are reinforced by his own sense of involvement and commitment. When the salesman acts in a 9,9 way, there is a good possibility that the customer will respond to him in kind.

Is all of this to say that a salesman should speak in terms of logic, facts, and data, from the initial prospective contact through to the closing? Does it mean that he assumes that each customer's personal motivations are 9,9 problem-solving ones, ignoring the actual fact that the customer's attitude at the point of initial contact may be 1,1; 5,5; 9,1; or 1,9?

No, it does not.

The best results are likely when the salesman is keenly aware of the customer's attitude, reading his every clue in order to understand the assumptions under which he is most likely to be responding. Should he ignore or violate these personal Grid attitudes, the salesman risks aborting his efforts. But if he uses the Grid to read the customer's frame of mind, he is in a position to work onward with him from where he is. If the customer is 1,1 disinterested, the question is, How can the salesman accept that and continue working in such a way as to get his participation and involvement before bringing him toward a 9,9 basis of mutuality? If he is 1,9 friendly and warm, the salesman can accept this trait and use it as a basis from which to get him more involved in understanding the product that is being described and demonstrated to him. If he is 5,5 tentative, taking confidence in the product's reputation rather than from any fundamental understanding of it, how can he be encouraged to develop convictions founded on product knowledge before making the buying decision? If he is 9,1 resistant and rejecting, seeing the salesman as out to get him by selling him something he doesn't need, how can his distrust of the salesman's motives be replaced with respect for the salesman's integrity and confidence in his product? The 9,9 approach yields clear and effective strategies for working constructively by accepting the customer for what he is and then building a 9,9 relationship with him. These are fundamental to sound selling.

chapter nine

On Being Helpful

An issue not yet mentioned but of overriding importance in any sound human relationship can now be discussed. It has been omitted thus far so you would first get a good grasp of the Grid. With the Grid as background, you are in a better position to see the fuller implications of the significance of this issue.

The issue is your helpfulness to the customer.

It is probably something of an oddity that in a book on selling you find the issue of "being helpful" raised to high importance. You can read many books on management, for example, and it would be most unusual to find this topic treated. It should be, but it isn't.

Why?

One answer stands out. It is that men with selling experience have been impressed by the appreciation received and the effect on their selling when they went beyond the formal business transaction to offer help where they could. Had they been giving help in the context of a more continuous and permanent relationship, they might not have recognized as clearly the sense of appreciation that the voluntary giving of help seems to generate. This fact is its own hazard because once the consequences of the act are recognized, the giving of help can be used as a a selling "tool." As you will see, when help is given in a false way, it frequently backfires because it is given insincerely or is used manipulatively.

Being helpful entails doing something for a customer which is above, beyond, and independent of the specific selling-purchasing transaction. It is adding something extra. Depending upon what conception the salesman has of being helpful, he may act in ways that contribute positively to his sales effectiveness, or he may place his effectiveness in peril. "Giving help" is intended to be understood in a broad sense. It may involve the giving of information or it may be a matter of providing your customer transportation from one place to another. It may involve buying a lunch, or helping a client by arranging tickets to the theater, or even an out-and-out gift. The emphasis is more on "giving" than on "helping," but since the two words are very close to each other, no distinction is drawn between them.

HELPFULNESS VIEWED FROM EACH GRID POSITION

Let's examine this matter of being helpful more closely. When a person is being genuinely helpful, he is giving someone an assist which otherwise would be absent. Possibly it is not something the recipient would miss if it had not been given. But the key is that a person is acting both because he sees an opportunity to be helpful and because he wants to contribute to another man's situation. The contribution is its own reward. It has no strings attached. This helpfulness may be quite commonplace such as simply passing along some new information which puts the recipient in a stronger position to understand some situation or event. He values it because he recognizes that it was unnecessary for you to give it to him. It adds to his understanding, and he knows you are not putting him under an obligation. The same applies when there is a very large contribution, such as aiding the recipient to seize an opportunity which would not otherwise have come to his attention but which is significant to him. This is 9,9 helpfulness. It is only possible to be helpful in this way when the person giving the help has a high concern for aiding other people in being more effective, for strengthening them, or in other ways making them "fuller"—more complete as persons.

This can be contrasted with 9,1 helpfulness. The person may search for and seize opportunities to give help, but always in such a way that it has strings attached. The recipient finds himself obligated as a result of accepting help. He recognizes that the person who gave it did so to produce an obligation, not to aid him.

1,9 helpfulness is of a still different character and quality. It is doing something for the person which he could very well do for himself, and he knows it. It makes the person who gives the help feel good, but it does not constructively aid the recipient or help him to become more effective. It does reflect a high concern for the person to whom it is given. But the person giving it is unwittingly making the receiver more dependent, even though it may not create a sense of obligation. He just gets accustomed to "letting George do it," probably accepting the help as a matter of course with very little sense of appreciation.

The 1,1 attitude toward giving help is, "Who needs it?" This neutral, noninvolved attitude is rationalized by the person who might have given the help saying to himself, "It wouldn't be appreciated if I did."

The 5,5 attitude is, "I'll scratch your back if you'll scratch mine." A classic example of this is found in a situation where vendors published special inflated price lists for one company purchasing agent so he could claim savings to top management after supposedly negotiating prices down. This kind of bargaining and trade-out rarely contributes to true effectiveness of selling. In nonbusiness situations its underlying commercial motivation tarnishes it and leads the customer to ask, "What's the angle?" Through "status" connections for getting hard-to-get theater tickets or ringside tables in expensive restaurants, the salesman expands his *quid pro quo* tactics.

These different basic attitudes toward giving help are observable all through the spectrum of human relationships. In and of themselves, they may have nothing to do with selling. They are fundamental to the way in which people act toward one another. But in another sense they have everything to do with selling.

The salesman, because he is not entrenched in the same situation as his customer, may be able to see the total situation in a clearer way than the customer who confronts his circumstances at short range. Sometimes the greatest help that the salesman can give is no more or less than a deep and genuine interest in a customer's problem. It is a relief for the customer to be able to talk it over with someone who is sympathetic and unbiased. It is better still when the salesman helps him to think the problem through and see the outlines of its solution.

This is particularly so when the salesman has made it his concern to know the customer and his situation by way of thorough preparation for understanding his problems. In addition to normal product sales and service matters, the salesman may be well situated to help the customer in unexpected ways which are quite separate from the product's potential contribution. These are helpful initiatives from the salesman's side but are not motivated by the "making a sale" consideration. Nevertheless, important gains can be incidentally realized. The salesman's positive interest in the customer is self-evident. It is constructive, not self-seeking and not part of a facade. The quality of his concern is the same, and the degree of concern is as high, as in his 9,9 sales approach. This is what builds confidence and trust. This is what increases the salesman's credibility with regard to his product.

CUSTOMER REACTIONS

How does the customer react to various other attitudes toward helpfulness?

The 9,1 way of being helpful—so as to create an obligation—does nothing to increase this salesman's credibility. The whole 9,1 approach betokens a pushing, sometimes blatantly exploitative attitude toward the customer. The salesman's sudden switch to apparent "helpfulness" carries overtones of falseness and deception which perceptive customers quickly notice. Others do not see the "strings attached" to his aid until after they have accepted it. What this can very easily do is to convert a positive attitude toward the salesman into resentment and long-lasting antagonism.

1,9 assistance caters to weakness in the person who receives it, because he has something done for him which he is fully capable of doing for himself. It is much like having an oversolicitous parent who, by her cloying attentions, deadens the child's initiative to act under his own steam.

The 1,1 attitude of indifference to where help could be given characterizes the salesman's numbness and uninvolvement in the human situation and further reduces the interest taken in him and his product.

The 5,5 form of helpfulness promotes a kind of continual balancing of the scales, with each party feeling that for propriety's sake he should give something in return for what he gets. It is more or less on the level of, "He had me out to lunch the last time he called—now that he's here again, it's my turn to pick up the check."

The giving of help is undoubtedly one of the more subtle and significant matters in any human relationship. A person should be aware of his own motivation for doing so, and of the likely negative consequences if it is done for the wrong reason. Equally, he should be clear as to the possible reciprocal benefits of doing so for sound reasons—sound from both the recipient's point of view and from his own.

There are many implications for effective selling in what has been said above, but let's examine just one. What would you expect a customer's reaction to you to be if you had already demonstrated one of these five attitudes toward being helpful and were now asking him to introduce you in a favorable manner to an acquaintance of his who might be a new sales prospect for you?

If you have been helpful in a 9,9 way, the prediction can confidently be made that he would not only be ready, he would be eager for his own acquaintances to become acquaintances of yours. If your giving of help had been of the 9,1 kind, he might mutter to himself, "I'll fix that s.o.b.," either giving you no leads at all or giving you ones that would lead you down the path to nowhere. If your attitude toward being helpful had been of a 1,9 quality, it is likely that he would already be feeling embarrassed and would wish to avoid creating similar embarrassment for any friend of his. He would probably defer, perhaps by indicating in a vague way that he would give it thought but with the real intention of turning away from your request. The 1,1 no-help attitude can be expected to promote a no-help attitude in return. The 5,5 way could well lead a customer into a bargaining attitude, asking you what would be in it for him, saying jokingly, "What's it worth by way of a discount?"

Whether the customer opens the gate, shuts doors, walks away, feels weak, or leaves the door ajar but not open when you request help from him is significantly a consequence of the way you gave him help.

chapter ten

On Being Deceptive

THERE ARE SALESMEN who are straightforward. Others are intention-
ally deceptive and manipulative. They work from behind a false front.
This kind of salesman is a facade strategist. But first, what does
"facade" mean?

Your company's office or store building has a front that faces a
street. It is what people see as they pass by. Maybe this front is fully
integrated with the rest of the building. It is what it appears to be.
There is no special ornamentation to give the entire building a
grandiose appearance. But the front of another building, as you may
be able to see it from above or behind, gives a false impression of the
character of the whole structure. Looking down from above, you can
see that a one-story building lies behind a three-story facade. What
looks like a palace from the front looks like a barn from behind. Such
a facade may trick you into going in; however this is a relatively harm-
less deception. It doesn't hurt anybody. And once inside you can walk
around and deal with people as they are, not as the phony front
indicated they would be.

A *personal* facade is something else again. It is carefully prepared but no less phony. Appearances and expressions, words, actions, and deeds are part of a facade strategy. Their purpose is trickery. They are calculated to be a front for concealing real intentions.

DIFFERENCES BETWEEN A GRID STYLE AND A FACADE

The "pure" theories of 9,1; 1,9; 1,1; 5,5; and 9,9 all share a basic attribute. They arise naturally from the particular sets of assumptions that salesmen adopt. The man who is employing one or more of these strategies is doing so because he believes that this is how he should be performing as a salesman or because it has become second nature with him. Although the consequences of his behavior might not be what he thinks they will be, he is nevertheless acting in a genuine way. He is not counterfeiting.[28]

A facade, on the other hand, is a cover for deception, intrigue, and trickery. In using a selling facade, the goal is to achieve, by indirect or by roundabout ways, a sales result that is *thought to be unattainable* if one's actual intentions are revealed or if pertinent facts and issues are faced up to. Thus a facade builder tries to avoid allowing his real intentions to appear on the surface. His approach is manipulative and devious.

To be sure, there are tactics and "sure-fire" sales techniques which numerous salesmen use as tools of their trade. Salesmen who have adopted 9,1 and 5,5 orientations are particularly attracted to them. But they are used as tools and gimmicks, as convenient tongs for extracting a purchase decision. There is a basic philosophy of honest purpose underlying them. They are not based on subterfuge.

KEY FEATURES OF FACADES

A general feature of any facade is that the facade strategist avoids revealing the contents of his own mind. He may give you the impression of being open and candid. This is precisely his intention! But his most purposeful thinking is hidden from you. There is little or nothing in what he says or does that prompts you to probe or question his motivations. They seem obvious. Yet you are looking at the facade and not seeing it for what it is.[29]

The reasons why people build up facades are as varied as their intentions. However, there are at least two broad categories of motivation which serve as the underpinnings of any facade. The one most widely described is the facade that covers a drive for mastery and control over people. You might think at first that this refers to a 9,1-oriented salesman who does not want to appear blatantly domineering when face to face with a customer. However, the authentic 9,1 orientation is to prove himself through *visible achievement*, usually in terms of high sales volume. Of course, the salesman with 9,1 attitudes also has a tendency to lose sight of the higher objective at times and be sidetracked into "proving" himself by his ability to win his argument with a customer. But he is open and honest with respect to his intentions. He really wants to win. In contrast, the facade builder's goal is private to himself. He gets his kicks from controlling and influencing people and events without their knowing it. High sales volume may be attained as a by-product of his manipulations, but this does not really grab him as it does the authentic 9,1. He is power-hungry and finds his jelly beans in "working" others on a ventriloquist/dummy basis.

A second category of facade motivation is related to the aim of being accepted and respected by the people with whom the salesman associates. Here also the facade strategist covers his true intentions. For example, he may put on a "tough guy" facade, an outer layer of what resembles 9,1 tough-mindedness, so as to cover his sensitivity and feelings of personal inadequacy. No matter what the true intention, however, it is typical for any facade strategist to resort to camouflage. He hides his actual motivation.

The facade he maintains from one time to another may or may not be consistent. His tactics may shift from one situation to another, depending on what he thinks is workable. The surface of a facade often has a 9,9 or 5,5 appearance; less frequently it shows itself as 9,1; 1,9; or 1,1.

Cloaking True Intentions

How can a facade strategist hide his true aims? There are many ways. One is simply not to get into deep-probing discussions with a customer. Keep the conversation at a surface level. Then there is less likelihood that he will be asked to make clear just what his position is. Another way of hiding is by not appearing to react to something which he notices in the situation. A 1,1-oriented salesman might likewise notice something and remain passive. The difference is that the facade builder takes the information and thinks about how he can use it. His seeming passivity is only on the surface, so that he will not alert the customer that he is on to something. If he did, the customer might ask, "What is it?" This would run counter to the facade builder's principle that "unshared knowledge is power at my disposal for manipulation" and might inadvertently reveal that his aims differed from the customer's.

A third way is to speak to a customer so as to reflect his own opinions back at him, without his noticing that the salesman's own opinions and attitudes are not being revealed. Similarly, reacting to a question with a counterquery can serve to deflect a customer probe. A fourth way does involve him in giving a reaction, but what the customer usually receives is a set of impressive-sounding half-truths which are phrased so as to gain his favor. Still another way of cloaking his true intentions is by telling an outright lie. He does not do this rashly; he always tries to lie in a way that can't be checked.

Building and Maintaining a Reputation

Not only does the facade builder avoid revealing his intentions, but he also works hard at creating a positive reputation for himself as a cover for his deceptive practices. Reputation building is a matter of speaking and acting consistently when in public and of connecting one's self with everything that is generally esteemed to be "good." A positive reputation serves the purpose of inducing people to put a favorable interpretation on all his actions as long as none of these is startlingly at variance with the rest. It gives smoothness and polish to the facade. The likelihood is increased that his actual motives and ways of operating will not be recognized. In this way he can appear to have integrity, as others are unable to see behind his outward appearances so as to sense what he really is.

Writers since Machiavelli have suggested how a reputation may be used to control, master, and dominate. The reputation is built around virtue, good deeds, and subscribing to popular causes. Many well-respected people are already engaged in helpful community activities, having no ulterior motives.[30] The facade builder joins in and gets to know them, sharing the goodwill. He works to bestow honor on all who excel. By this means, he identifies himself with excellence. He also gains benefit from praising others—a tactic that will be examined in more detail later on. Another cover-up is to express lofty convictions and socially valued ideals; to be for the good, true, and beautiful. Genuinely humanitarian people speak and act in this way, and so, ostensibly, does he. His surface behavior frequently cannot be distinguished from that which is motivated by valid intentions. As he strengthens his impressive social and church connections, it becomes possible for him to use the names, activities, and business or official functions of well-respected persons to bolster his own actions. By joining these kinds of community activities, many entry points with prospects also become available to him that otherwise might be closed doors. Therein lie his true intentions. When the facade builder can name-drop or enlist the support of one or more opinion molders, he has widely extended the scope for undercover work to further his personal ambitions.

Whatever tactics are being used, the strategy in facade building is the same. It is to ensure that others perceive the salesman's aims as genuine and honorable when, in fact, they are devious and manipulative. When customers and others have sufficient confidence in him to be willing to relax their usual vigilance and omit normal precautions, the way is open for him to influence them and to obtain personal authority or sales results on a disproportionate scale to his actual competence and contribution.

MOTIVATING AND CONTROLLING CUSTOMERS

The facade strategist recognizes two principal ways of motivating and controlling other people. A demonstrated concern for the other person, with expressions of approval for what he is doing or saying, is a positive way of influencing him. Criticism, or any other way of speaking or acting so as to reduce his self-esteem, is a negative and punishing form of motivation. A deceptive salesman is carefully selective in using these two options and the alternatives within each.

Praise

The clever use of praise is a key factor. This salesman's use of praise may give some appearance of 1,9 to his facade, in that a friendly concern for the customer may be read into the close attention and unqualified support given to the customer's points of view, with readiness to discuss any general topic that the customer brings up. However, in 1,9 the concern is a genuine one. A 1,9-oriented salesman is interested in people, liking them and wanting to be liked by them. The facade strategist wants to use them. "You can catch more flies with honey than with vinegar," is a well-known adage that fits the thinking of the facade strategist.

He is lavish with praise and approbation. Compliments make the customer feel important. They build up his self-esteem. The person who has been made to feel praiseworthy also comes to like and admire the individual from whom the praise originated. Praise buys influence over the customer, and hence, a sale. It is an exchange: the customer is made to feel good, and he responds. Whether there was anything *deserving* of praise is an irrelevant question to this salesman. But he knows that he should, in some degree, be discriminating. He does not want to go too far, so as to endanger his credibility. He ponders, How far is *too* far? and has a clear idea in dealing with each customer of the limit beyond which the amount of praise he might give would be detected as obvious flattery. In all things, he avoids being obvious. By the same token, he is careful not to be led astray by flattery of himself by others.

Concern for Customers

Showing concern for the other person's needs and respecting his opinions is a more subtle form of influencing him than is direct praise. To a deceptive salesman, it is important throughout the sales interview that he should be coming across to the customer as one who is genuinely interested in him and in what he has to say. Ways in which this is done vary from being a good supportive listener, who grunts approval on cue, to never telling or suggesting to a customer that he is wrong, to avoiding arguments or any hint of opposition. As one person said, "I make it a point to find out what a person is most interested in so that I can ask questions and get him to talk. In this way, not only does he tend to be put in a positive frame of mind, but also it helps him to feel important. Because he is friendly toward me, he is more likely to buy what I want him to later on." The facade strategist need not risk incurring a customer's dislike by setting him straight on some matter. The customer's mistaken opinions can be used, in a number of subtle ways, to bring him under control. Like a judo expert, the deceptive salesman uses the other person's errors as his own opportunities. So on the surface, he appears sympathetic to the customer's ideas and opinions. To a customer who assumes that the salesman is well intentioned, these manifestations of concern for him will probably have 9,9 or 1,9 overtones.

A 1,9 Facade

Some very deep and extensive manipulations can be carried out under cover of a 1,9 facade, but there is at least one pattern which is relatively simple and easily recognizable. This is when a salesman initiates and fosters a social relationship, apparently for no other reason than liking the person involved. His real purpose, however, is to achieve a hidden aim. For instance, on a social visit, there is general conversation ranging across several topics which include the other person's health, family composition, retirement plans, and so on. Only after he feels he is fully accepted as a friend, maybe days or weeks later, does the salesman broach the subject of his real interest, which is to sell the other person some insurance.

This kind of 1,9 facade seems to derive its motivation from fear of offending. To reduce this fear, the salesman himself has taken out an "insurance policy" of personal acceptance—paying his premium by being nice—as a cover for his real intentions. In Asia this facade is labeled "long toes." The salesman's extreme sensitivity to the thought of being rejected or "stepped on" has driven him to establish a personal relationship as the setting within which to realize his aims.

A 9,9 Facade

When a 9,9 facade is being employed, all elements of the Sales Grid style except integrity are present. Data are presented objectively, the customer is brought into participation and helped to analyze and define his requirements, and a product or program is satisfactorily fitted to them. Within the interview situation there has been full candor, and consensus has been achieved. But there is something outside of it that is hidden from the customer.

Representatives of an insurance company call on a prominent citizen. They explain that their company has not previously written policies in this city or state but is now beginning to develop business here. They present and explain their programs to him. From the personal data he provides, they draw up sample proposals for a comprehensive coverage which he at present lacks. He checks these over and is favorably impressed. The premium rates are advantageous in comparison to what he would be quoted by any other company that operates in the area. Coverage and benefits are equal or superior. The representatives state that they have been authorized to write a very limited number of policies at reduced premium rates in this initial phase of new business development. He signs up and they leave after mentioning that they hope he will recommend their company to his friends. He says, "Sure, I will." It is a spontaneous, casual gesture on his part.

What the salesmen have not told him is that he was selected as a target person to be signed up and thenceforward to be used as part of the company's sales promotion campaign strategy in this region. From now on, his name will be put before every prospect who is likely to be impressed by it. He will be referred to as a well-satisfied policyholder and, implicitly, as one who endorses the soundness of the company and of every deal that its salesmen negotiate.

Criticism

To the facade strategist, negative forms of motivation appear dangerous. Criticism of any aspect of a customer's situation, even of a competitor's product that he has purchased or is considering, is ruled out. For example, under one school of thought a person may justifiably feel critical yet should not directly criticize another, because men are seen as emotional rather than logical. Criticism can easily fire up these emotions, setting off the "powder keg of pride." [31] The suggestion, then, is that direct criticism is much too dangerous for an individual to play with if he wants to win friends and influence people. By abstaining from criticism, the negative reactions that could ensue are avoided. The tacit deception is of no consequence.

What is manipulative here? The manipulative feature is that all facts and opinions that might be unpleasing are withheld. When this is done, the person to whom these facts and opinions could have proved instructive is misled.

Initiative and Perseverance

A characteristic of the facade strategist is that he acts with initiative and continues to pursue his aim until success is ensured. Although it might not appear so on the surface, in his action he is tough-minded. He acts quickly when he sees an advantage to be gained. He does not become sentimentally involved with people, even though his feigned interest almost parallels what could be for real. Rather, he is able to use people and to make alliances which are easily and quickly set aside as the occasion demands. By staying uninvolved, he is not likely to have conflicting motives and can concentrate on the end to be attained. He does not easily let obstacles throw him. If one approach does not succeed, he draws back and then tries another tack until his objective is realized.

In a like manner he is not daunted by difficult selling problems or by any stresses that the customer imposes. Yet, he is not closed-minded. He is responsive to new facts and new opportunities which might provide him with additional leverage. Inwardly, he is not likely to be restricted in his thinking by respect for company rules and traditional practices, as full observance of these would often-times limit his scope. However, when it is to his advantage, he personifies and upholds the status quo.

Thus, in building and maintaining a personal facade, the salesman:
1. Is lavish with praise and approbation
2. Demonstrates a concern for people
3. Avoids direct criticism

4. Never gives up, but knows when to withdraw so as to come in again from another direction

In these ways he avoids antagonizing customers and others, and stimulates their willingness to go along with him.

WHY DO SOME SALESMEN EMPLOY FACADES?

A few of the ways in which facade builders screen off their personal motivation from customers and others have been illustrated. Control and mastery of customers have to be achieved through persuasion and acceptance. The salesman knows it is not practicable to coerce them. But in effect, his way is to use people like nonhuman objects: to set them up for processing, brush them aside if they are in his way, carom them into the pocket with his cue ball. The facade disguises these manipulations. Why does he act in this way?

You may think that he goes to a lot of trouble for no obvious reason. So he does. For what? you may ask. Does he possess a mystical secret of exploitative selling that will raise him to a position of wealth and power? What is he gaining in terms of sales results, effectiveness in working with customers, personal prestige, or anything else he is driving for?

The answer to these questions is that he believes his personal objective would be unattainable if he did behave more openly. To the extent that he is pursuing power and some personal pleasure in manipulating others, the means he has chosen for gaining these ends may be the only practical one. Most people would recoil if they knew of these intentions. They would oppose his efforts. The facade permits him to select and pursue his personal goals in private. It screens these activities from outside observation and so prevents resistance—that would reduce his power—from developing. The important thing to note is that the facade strategist's rationale for his conduct—the attainment of "super power" or super sales that he believes can be gained in no other way—influences his whole approach and everything he does. It is a central assumption that is as potent in governing *his* behavior as any of the assumptions that undergird the various Grid styles.

There are at least two reasons for building up and maintaining a facade.

Disregard of Social Ethics

The facade builder does not value mutual trust between the customer and himself in its own right. Yet the appearance of trustfulness is important. Through creating an impression that candor, helpfulness, and honest dealing are the central features of his approach, he can achieve his personal goals more easily. On the plane of social ethics, in consequence, shortcuts are taken to the desired end. The facade strategist is not governed by commonly accepted rules for maintaining social morality.

Attainment of Goals beyond One's Capability

Another motive for facade building is when a salesman strives to achieve a goal which he believes is beyond his intrinsic capability and skill to achieve directly. By employing a facade to hide tricky and deceitful maneuvers, the objectives he is striving for can be gained. The end sought justifies the means used for getting it.

The tragic aspect is that, if his assumptions were different—if he believed that he *could* achieve excellent sales results and satisfy his personal ambitions through straightforward selling effort—his energy and resourcefulness would most likely guarantee outstanding success for him as a salesman and as a future executive. Admittedly, some facade strategists get a distorted thrill out of "living dangerously" and achieving by complex maneuvers what could have been reached by a direct approach. But there are relatively few of these. Most of the salesmen who have adopted deceptive selling strategies lack confidence in their own abilities and so may be deceiving *themselves*.

Self-deception Concerning One's Own Motivation

Facade-type behavior sometimes appears when the underlying motivation is hidden even from the salesman himself. He literally doesn't know he is putting on a front. Not only are others deceived, he also deceives himself. Psychiatry and clinical psychology have described tricks of the mind. These are tricks by which a person's motivations are unclear to himself; they can't be identified by him or described to others. If directly confronted with his own self-deceptions, he would deny them. *Rationalization* is an example: the person is quick to provide plausible, creditable, but untrue motives for his conduct. Really he is kidding himself. He may *project* his own motives, arguing that all salesmen have to trick their customers into purchasing something. Another example is when a person *compensates* for failure in one area of his life by striving to demonstrate success in another area.

Facade-type behavior may be caused by any of these factors or by a mixture of them. To complicate matters further, the behavior may contain components of the pure theories as well. Presence of the latter only adds to the subtlety of the person's self-deception as well as to his deception of others.

SUMMARY

A sales facade may be adopted by a person who seeks to mask his pursuit of personal and private goals. Insofar as his observable behavior appears well intentioned and his true motivation is hidden, he is likely to be seen as 5,5; 9,9; 1,9; 9,1; or as adopting a mixture of different Grid strategies. Since his tactics vary to take advantage of the opportune situation and people's weaknesses, it may be difficult to pinpoint the facade builder except by tracking his activities over a time span. The utilization of facades to cloak intentions constitutes a personal barrier to the achievement of 9,9 relationships with both customers and colleagues.

A facade strategist can be highly successful. But he is a potential Achilles heel to customer and company. The lack of integrity inherent in a facade means that the company is being represented to customers by a salesman who lacks trustworthiness. This kind of untrustworthiness is likely to lead into shady deals which can have a tremendous boomerang effect when either a customer or the company eventually discovers that he has been taking advantage of them.

chapter eleven

The Customer Grid

THE CUSTOMER HAS BEEN in the wings in the previous chapters which examined salesmen's Sales Grid styles. Now he needs to come on stage.

FACTORS INFLUENCING A CUSTOMER'S DECISION

What are the factors which act on the customer independently of his Grid style in any purchasing situation? They are many and varied. Four stand out. Each is an important consideration in how you plan your sales presentation and interact with the customer.

Ability to Buy

A customer listens to your presentation through his pocketbook. Of course, "pocketbook" means what he has in it plus his access to credit. If it is empty, he cannot make a positive decision to purchase, no matter what you say. If it is loaded, this factor does not impede his listening. However, the pocketbook may be in someone else's possession; that is, the customer may not have the power of purchasing decisions.

Desire

Customers desire things in varying degrees. Their desires are related to their practical and emotional needs and the problems they face that need resolution. The desire for a product can be intense and all-consuming. The customer thinks of nothing else. At the other end of the desire spectrum are negative motivations. He actively rejects a product as detrimental rather than beneficial to him in meeting his needs or solving a problem. In between is a neutral position of disengagement. His mind is in neither forward nor reverse gear so far as desire is concerned. The desire may be well supported by reasoning or it may be of a more general nature—a desire for something to solve a personal or business problem without knowing what it is that would satisfy his desire.

Product Knowledge

The customer's knowledge of your product can range from nonexistent through a general comprehension of it to an expert's proficiency in understanding it. Or, the customer can be misinformed about it. If he is ignorant about your product, he lacks motivation to possess it. If he is well informed, he may already approve of it or feel highly resistant to buying it. Of course, product knowledge spreads out into knowledge of competitors' products as well as your own. Then, if the customer's knowledge is full, he may be making a comparison judgment as you interact with him, rather than simply evaluating your product solely on its own merits.

Expectations

A fourth consideration that influences a customer's reactions is his expectations. He may have high expectations that the product will satisfy his desire, or his expectations may be low in the sense that he cannot see any possibility that the product you represent will meet his needs and desires.

These four: ability to buy, desire, knowledge, and expectations, are key factors in the customer's mind. The greatest likelihood of your making a sale is when all of these are strong, positive, and valid. Then the customer can pay, he has a desire he wants satisfied, he has accurate knowledge of your product, and he has valid expectations that it will meet his desires. The most difficult conditions under which to make a sale are when all factors are negative. He is unable to pay. He has no desire, no knowledge, and contrary expectations. The majority of customers are somewhere between these extremes. This is why your effectiveness as a salesman consists of several aspects. One is in helping him see how he might be able to afford your product. Another is in testing whether he has an actual or potential desire which your product can satisfy, and in providing the knowledge essential for seeing how your product would meet his desire. Finally, you should ensure that his expectations for what your product can do for him are realistic. Your interview with him is a unique situation. You may have further interviews later, but the dynamics will have changed by then. It is in the here-and-now, and from moment to moment, that you are confronting whatever he has in mind. Conversely, he is responding to your thoughts and attitudes as he perceives them.

A sales interview that acknowledges these key influencing factors cannot be programmed along *attention-interest-desire-action* lines but has a creative interpersonal character and quality. The reason is that in any particular situation these factors can combine with one another in varied and complex ways. They present you with a different situation each time you meet another customer, or the same customer at various times. This is one reason why every customer is a distinctive individual in comparison with every other. If you are to be creative and genuinely flexible, you have to figure out—either as a basis for prospecting or conducting a sales interview—where a customer stands on all these factors. Whether you recognize it or not, you're undoubtedly making mental judgments about where he stands as you meet and interact with him. What really makes selling challenging is that you are making these inferences through his Grid style and through your own as well. You are trying to adjust your sales position along all these mental planes.

Perhaps the best way to show how customers' Grid styles operate in selling situations is to study each major Grid position on the assumption that a customer is reasonably capable of paying, has a moderate desire, possesses essential but not complete information, and has expectations which are at least partially realistic.

THE 9,1-ORIENTED CUSTOMER

What are the general reactions of a 9,1-oriented customer during a sales presentation? He has a high desire to make a purchase but little concern for you as a salesman. Thus, he wants to satisfy himself that your product is what *he* wants; he won't think twice about rejecting it if he believes it is wrong. He is likely to shield his desires, data, and thought processes from you to avoid getting sucked into making a purchase he does not want. Thus, he might play down his desire, indicating that he is not particularly interested in what you have to sell. He may assert or imply that your competitors are quoting lower prices than you are. He overplays his knowledge to give you the impression that he is better informed than he is. His expectations are on the negative side, distrusting that your product will meet his hidden desires.

The 9,1-oriented Salesman

What happens if the salesman—who is 9,1-oriented too—responds to the customer in this way? Under these circumstances, the interview becomes a battle of wits. The karate match is on. Each contestant is looking for an opening. The salesman's purpose is to turn him on; the customer's, to stay turned off or at least to give that impression so that he's not seen as "knuckling under." It is a situation where someone is going to emerge the winner and someone else the loser. Unless the customer has some basis for winning, for example, if he is satisfied he's beaten the salesman down on some minor point or other, the salesman is unlikely to capture the sale through proving him wrong in a debating match. There can be no consensus; the sale can only be made if each of the two can convince himself, for reasons unknown to the other, that he has "won."

The 1,9-oriented Salesman

This salesman is overly sensitive to the 9,1 customer's negative attitude. He may initially try to respond to the radiated hostility with friendliness but very quickly retreats, with hurt feelings, and starts searching for a way to get out of the situation.

The 1,1-oriented Salesman

This is probably the most brief of all salesman encounters when the customer's attitude is initially negative. The 1,1-oriented salesman takes his refusal at face value although the other's hostile faultfinding and provocative statements roll off his back like water off a duck. These have no effect on his emotions, but they signal to him that all bets are off. Mentally he throws up his hands saying, "What's the use; he doesn't want to buy."

The 5,5-oriented Salesman

The 5,5-oriented salesman is not as quickly discouraged as the person operating under 1,1 assumptions. His inclination is to continue through his pat routine, attempting to stay on course when interruptions and objections occur. He ignores some, gives "Yes, but . . ." answers to others, and tries to forestall future objections by expanding his presentation to answer them in advance. He will strive to continue up to the point when the customer makes his dissatisfaction and impatience openly known and terminates discussion.

The 9,9-oriented Salesman

Most probably, this salesman has already built his knowledge of the customer in terms of his ability to buy, his desire, and his general level of knowledge and expectations, as well as developed some prior understanding of his dominant Grid style. He anticipates the likelihood of the customer acting in a provocative manner and of having a negative, skeptical attitude. His first point of entry is to provide general knowledge of his product to get the customer's initial reaction. Then he introduces easy questions of a sort that do not suggest to the customer that he is being pressured to admit his ignorance. The purpose is to try to capture his interest by first stimulating his thinking. The customer's queries and possible negative reactions provide the salesman clues as to what additional knowledge the other man needs to comprehend the product fully. Next, he gets the customer to talk about any problems he may have in the general area to which the product relates. It is at this point that the salesman is in an excellent position to present the product's benefits and get the customer to see how they fit his situation. By getting him to test his knowledge and desires simultaneously, he develops a basis for making sure that the customer's expectations of the product's meeting his desires are realistic. In this way, the 9,9 salesman helps the 9,1 customer to convince himself that the product is suitable for him.

By way of summary: The 9,1 customer reactions are most likely to throw off the attempts by salesmen operating from 1,1; 1,9; and 5,5 approaches. A gambler might figure the outcome of the battle when 9,1 meets 9,1 at about 6-to-4 in the customer's favor. The 9,9 salesman has the greatest likelihood of successful closing.

THE 1,9-ORIENTED CUSTOMER

This customer, with a low concern for making a purchase interacting with a high human concern for the salesman, would leave no doubt about his pleasure in being visited. He may overstate his interest in the product and desire for it, so as not to offend the salesman. He does not mind revealing his lack of product knowledge and is ready to believe the salesman's propositions without requesting proof. He punctuates a presentation with affirmative shakes of his head. He is easily persuaded that the product will satisfy his desires; even though, if he were to consider it by himself, he might soon see that it would not. In a salesman's presence, however, he is suggestible and easily influenced.

The 9,1-oriented Salesman

This salesman sees the 1,9-oriented customer as a pushover. He recognizes that here is someone who can be induced to buy readily and quickly. The salesman's tactic then is to short-circuit his sales presentation on the knowledge side and to hammer on the benefits by showing how the product will satisfy the customer's desires. Since the salesman is unlikely to probe the customer for a realistic assessment of his situation and what his needs actually are, he probably raises the customer's expectations to an exaggeratedly high level regarding what the product will do for him. The chances are a purchase will be made, even though the customer will probably be disappointed with the result at a later time. But he won't complain; rather, he will avoid having an unpleasant followup discussion with the salesman and will look for others to satisfy his future desires. So he is unlikely to become an established long-term account.

The 1,9-oriented Salesman

This situation is one of mutual delight and admiration. The customer's warmth and congeniality strike a responsive chord with the salesman. However, the low concern for making a sale meets a low concern for making a purchase. Thus, the interview turns into a charming social visit, flowing along rivulets of joint interests unrelated to the purpose of the visit. Over the long haul, it is likely to turn out to be a successful relationship. On each successive call the customer is inclined to want to do something generous for the salesman. This means he tends to purchase even though his desires may not be high or his expectations realistically founded. However, if he is dissatisfied with the product at a later time, he is unlikely to be displeased with the salesman; he is more likely to blame himself for not asking about the other products his friend had to offer. He may be counted on by the salesman as an established account, for the customer looks forward to additional enjoyable visits.

The 1,1-oriented Salesman

The 1,1-oriented salesman is likely to misread the clues in the 1,9 customer's behavior toward him as a person. Rather than accurately interpreting the customer's desire to be liked, he sees him as operating more out of social protocol. Nevertheless, he accurately interprets the customer's low desire for making a purchase since the customer does not initiate any purchasing moves and the salesman is not likely to either. The interview, while it may drag on for a while, ends with the salesman's saying he may call again and leaving without attempting to close a sale.

The 5,5-oriented Salesman

The presentation of a 5,5-oriented salesman elicits positive responses from the customer. While the salesman might not fully satisfy the customer's desire to be liked, he would probably bring about a successful closing. The customer wants to say Yes and avoid saying No and therefore will most likely respond affirmatively to the salesman's queries. The 5,5-oriented salesman's difficulties may begin when he tries to close. If, all along, the customer is unwilling to buy, he may still say Yes up to the point of closing. From that moment on, though, rather than coming out with a No, he is most likely to try to defer. In this way, he can avoid being negative but yet not consummate the purchase. If the salesman presses forward at this point, instead of taking the deferral as a real need for delay, he will most probably be able to get him to buy there and then. If the customer's expectations of a product are not fulfilled later on, though, he will blame the salesman rather than himself.

The 9,9-oriented Salesman

This salesman quickly senses the risks that are inherent in swift and easy closing. Rather than starting with a knowledge-based presentation as he might for a 9,1 customer, he begins by probing the customer's desires in order to gain a deeper understanding of the needs and wants that the customer so easily believes the product can satisfy. He might anticipate finding that the customer's desires are more impulse-based than predicated on realistic assessment. His job then is to supplement the customer's knowledge of the product, ensuring that his expectations of its capability to fulfill his desires are well grounded. Any unrealistic expectations on the customer's part will be identified and pointed out to him. The salesman is able to communicate his friendliness to the customer while at the same time clarifying his needs and helping him to understand more about the product. He does this without making the customer embarrassed about his own lack of thoroughness. The difficult point is that a 1,9 customer is prepared to listen and assent to whatever information is provided. So the salesman needs to test continuously to make sure that the customer is not past the point of saturation—that he *really* comprehends what the salesman is saying and is relating each additional point to what has been explained previously. This is a potential pitfall, because a 9,9 salesman's enthusiasm for product knowledge as the basis of a decision can carry him past the correct needs of the situation.

In summary, then, the 1,9 customer is an easy person to sell. A salesman can make a successful closing under any Grid style except 1,1.

The basis for closing under 9,1; 5,5; and 1,9 might not be realistic, and should the product fail to measure up to the high expectations for it, a 1,9 customer tends to avoid the salesman in the future and turn to other sources where he is not so likely to be disappointed.

THE 1,1-ORIENTED CUSTOMER

A 1,1-oriented customer, with low concern for making a sound purchase and low concern for the salesman, would quickly communicate his disinterest. The resulting inertia places full weight on the salesman to carry the discussion and to provide the momentum if the sale is to be made.

The 9,1-oriented Salesman

The 9,1-oriented salesman has a great opportunity to continue his monologue uninterrupted. He reels off his product knowledge and selling points with little reason to stop. His customer's lack of response is unlikely to make him feel uneasy. He continues without testing whether the customer is with him. Because of the force of his presentation, a 1,1-oriented customer's inclination is to withdraw even further and find ways to retreat from the situation. If it is possible for him to do so, he finds an excuse to get up and leave—"I'm late for the meeting . . ."—and the 9,1 salesman is unsuccessful in making a close. However, if the 9,1 salesman can stay alongside him long enough, he has a fairly good chance of browbeating him into signing on the dotted line. Later on, though, the order may be canceled, ostensibly by the purchasing agent's boss or on some other excuse.

The 1,9-oriented Salesman

The salesman is distressed at the 1,1 customer's lack of responsiveness to him. He might keep searching for evidence of mutual social interest in terms of which to build a relationship. Finding none, he would present his product in a weak and disheartened manner, not anticipating a successful closing. He creates so little pressure or persuasiveness that he is unlikely to get one. He responds to a "not interested," with "Thanks, it was a pleasure to meet you," as he takes his leave.

The 1,1-oriented Salesman

The slightest sales result imaginable is when 1,1 visits with 1,1. "Here I am again—do you have something for me?" "No." "Okay, so long." If the answer is "Yes," the response is, "Okay, I'll take your order."

The 5,5-oriented Salesman

The salesman quickly recognizes the key difference between the 1,9- and the 1,1-oriented customer. The former responds affirmatively to the programmed questions that are interspersed in the 5,5 sales presentation. A 1,1 customer responds with a grunt or silence. If the salesman continues through his presentation and closing sales steps, rather than taking silences as an indication of "zero interest" and becoming discouraged, he has an even chance of making a successful close.

The 9,9-oriented Salesman

To overcome 1,1 apathy, the salesman works with knowledge and enthusiasm to see whether he can spark an interest. His initial queries are briefly phrased and aim at eliciting some yes/no answers to determine whether pickup is occurring. His objective is to activate an interest or locate a foundation of understanding upon which he can build. He does not take the customer's 1,1 dominant style at face value but tries to activate a 9,9 backup style as the basis for moving toward a close.

The 9,9-oriented salesman is most likely to promote a valid sale with the 1,1-oriented customer. The reason is that he works with him in order to activate a backup style in terms of which the customer can begin reasoning with him toward a sound purchasing decision. A 9,1- or 5,5-oriented salesman has an even chance of promoting a close with the 1,1-oriented customer. A 1,9 or a 1,1 is unlikely to strike even one spark of interest.

THE 5,5-ORIENTED CUSTOMER

The 5,5-oriented customer expects to be treated in a diplomatic way. He does not want to be challenged to think deeply. He wants a solution to his problem that he can accept with confidence, one that is consistent with what others have judged it best to do in a similar situation. He will allow the salesman's confidence to move him from tentativeness as long as what is being presented does not go against conventional thinking. He can be expected to interrupt and raise objections to any aspects of the presentation which might make him feel uneasy. Because his desires are rooted in conformity to the norms and values of social groups to which he belongs—in terms of "what other people think"—the salesman may sometimes have difficulty in understanding how this prospect views his own situation and in penetrating to the source of his desires.

The 9,1-oriented Salesman

The force and drive of a 9-1-oriented salesman's presentation put some reinforcement into the tentativeness with which the 5,5 customer enters the selling situation. However, there are two ways in which a 9,1-oriented salesman's approach may make a negative impact. One is that he may brush aside the 5,5 customer's questions, interruptions, and objections in an abrupt and unfeeling way. The customer may recoil from this kind of treatment and become resistant to the salesman's efforts. Even though a product may meet his needs, he might be so piqued as to refuse to buy. The second pitfall that a 9,1-oriented salesman may encounter is that his presentation of the product's benefits and the needs that it can fulfill might not square with the customer's expectations of what this kind of product should be able to do for him. This is because the salesman is unlikely to probe in depth to understand the source of the 5,5 customer's desires. He can run into resistance that he might not be able to understand since he is encountering the "expectations" of other people that the 5,5 customer values.

The 1,9-oriented Salesman

The 1,9-oriented salesman does not inspire confidence in a tentative 5,5 customer because he, the salesman, is likely to become discouraged under questioning, and to wilt. The customer may lose confidence in the product as a result of the poor sales presentation. However, the salesman's sociable attitudes and personal interest in the customer are reassuring to him. The result may be that the salesman wins a friend and loses a sale.

The 1,1-oriented Salesman

The 1,1 tendency to answer questions in a turned-off mechanical way does nothing to stir a 5,5 customer's interest. The salesman's lack of interest and enthusiasm does not inspire sufficient confidence in him to result in a purchase.

The 5,5-oriented Salesman

This situation is where the 5,5 salesman finds his most natural success. A 5,5-oriented customer is easy to deal with and a joy to sell. They are both tuned to and respond to the same kind of signals. The customer's lack of interest in deep product knowledge fits the salesman's superficial level. The 5,5-oriented customer's desires which are formulated in conventional terms are consistent with the salesman's tried-and-true strategies.

The 9,9-oriented Salesman

The 5,5-oriented customer is responsive to a 9,9 presentation because the salesman responds to the customer as a person but is not oversolicitous. He can provoke the customer's innate readiness to participate and to be involved. Being knowledgeable about his product, he is also able to steer the 5,5 customer's interest into thinking along problem-solving channels. He ferrets out the source of the customer's desires and can add confidence to the customer by aiding him to gain insight into how the product will meet these desires and give him true satisfaction.

The 5,5 customer can respond in a problem-solving way to a 9,9 sales orientation. He also finds himself in rhythm with the 5,5 sales strategy. The 9,1-oriented salesman can be successful if he does not step too hard on the customer's psychic toes. The 1,9- and 1,1-oriented salesmen are not sufficiently forceful to promote confidence in the customer that a decision to purchase would be an appropriate one.

THE 9,9-ORIENTED CUSTOMER

A customer with a high concern for making a sound purchase and high concern for the salesman is accustomed to thinking logically in a way that cuts through unsupported assertions and emotion-laden attempts to persuade him. When a salesman is not on his wavelength, he is prepared to exercise leadership and bring the discussion up to a problem-solving level. He recognizes the personal limitations that some salesmen have, but is unwilling to purchase in terms of those limitations—either on the basis of partial knowledge or of unsound relationships.

The 9,1-oriented Salesman

The salesman's emphasis on product knowledge stimulates the 9,9 customer's interest in a sound purchase. The customer can be expected to query the salesman at points where the presentation does not square with his own factual knowledge or assessment of his situation. The 9,1 salesman's attempt to brush aside or diminish the importance of these checking points is met with customer persistence in having them answered. When he is challenged, the 9,1 salesman's inclination is to convert the previously objective interview into a win-lose argument. He is likely to be disappointed at his inability to provoke a more heated discussion with this customer, who keeps his cool and continues probing for facts and data. If he is unable to make progress under these conditions, the 9,1 salesman may throttle down and become more factual in providing explanations where he is requested to, or to acknowledge his inability to provide the needed information immediately. The salesman's attempts to display product benefits and to arouse desire only meet with success when he can show that the product really fits. As he follows his usual approach, he is not likely to add to the customer's current understanding of his own situation or to aid him in seeing it in a novel or different light. Thus, if the salesman's product explanations jibe with the customer's self-formulated requirements, he can expect to make a sale. If not, the salesman is unlikely to possess the flexibility of alternative ways of viewing the customer's situation so as to make it possible to come to a successful closing.

The 1,9-oriented Salesman

This salesman is unlikely to meet success when confronted with a 9,9 customer. His lack of in-depth knowledge of his product and his readiness to skate along on superficial niceties are factors which do not meet the problem-solving requirements of the customer's purchasing decision. The salesman does not find the situation unattractive, yet he is unlikely to understand either why this customer does not respond to his friendliness by purchasing, or why it is, after he has been sent back to his company with a list of points that the customer wants clarified, that his own boss gets in touch with the customer and maybe closes a sale.

The 1,1-oriented Salesman

When 1,1 assumptions guide his thinking, a salesman can anticipate failure in dealing with a 9,9-oriented customer. His superficial presentation and the shallowness of his knowledge, which becomes evident as the customer probes, simply do not earn respect. The customer requires that his purchase will be a sound one and will meet the needs of his particular situation.

The 5,5-oriented Salesman

This salesman finds the going tough with the 9,9 customer even though the chances are about even that he might end up with a sale. The reason is that his pat routine is frequently interrupted and the depth of his product knowledge is tested from moment to moment. This is not the destructive interrogation of a 9,1 customer. He can expect the 9,9 customer to help him by probing in constructive ways for the product's strengths and limitations and by aiding the salesman to understand the customer's situation and the extent to which the product meets his desires.

The 9,9-oriented Salesman

The salesman who is oriented in the 9,9 way finds his greatest personal reward from selling to a 9,9-oriented customer. The order of the presentation is difficult to predict, but a successful outcome is most likely. The salesman knows his product; his orientation is to sell solutions. These match the customer's requirements for knowledge and his method of continually testing his problem against what the salesman offers. The importance of realistic expectations regarding what the product will or will not do is equally clear to both salesman and customer, and both search for the basis of creating valid expectations as a basis of decision. These reciprocal attitudes make participation and involvement a natural basis for give-and-take, making it easy for the salesman to indicate particular product limitations without feeling that he is losing the sale. They make it possible also for the customer to accept limitations as realistic and inevitable.

In summary, the salesman with a 9,9 approach has the greatest chance of meeting the mind of a 9,9 customer. The reason is that each man's problem-solving orientation matches the other's. Every one of the other Sales Grid styles lacks one or more of the essential ingredients of problem solving. However, out of these, the salesman who has the greater reservoir of product knowledge (which often is commensurate with his degree of concern for making a sale) is more likely to be successful than the one who has less. Those with low concern for making a sale, regardless of how much concern they show for the customer, will run the greatest risk of failure.

CONCLUSIONS

Sales skill in making a clear presentation of what your product can and cannot do in discussing how it may serve the customer, and in creating valid expectations on his part, cannot be expected to overcome resistance to a shoddy product or to move your product when your competitor's is far better and your customer knows it. But where sales skill can help you is when your product is what the customer needs and when other products enjoy no vast superiority over your own. They can also help you when your product is better than those of your competitor's. The reason is that while the superiority of your product may be obvious to you, it may not be to your customer. Even so, no matter how much a customer wants your product or how good it is, poor sales skill can kill a deal.

This study of how sales styles and customer styles fit together or are mismatched provides a basis for understanding why certain kinds of salesmen are successful with some customers and not with others. Finally, it provides a basis for understanding the "star," the salesman who seems capable of being successful with a wide range of different customers. Fortunately, the assumptions on which Grid styles are based are ones that a person can learn about and adopt. Alternative assumptions that might strengthen your selling effectiveness also can be learned. How you might shift from one set of assumptions to another is the focus of the next two chapters.

chapter twelve

Communicating with the Customer

THE SALESMAN AND THE CUSTOMER arrive or fail to arrive at a success-ful closing through talking with each other. To the customer, your readiness to understand him and his situation is all important. His objections and complaints, for example, are at the very heart of his feelings. The same is true about his participation and involvement—how willing you, the salesman, are to have him take an active part in thinking along with you, analyzing what the product can do for him. Regardless of *his* Grid style, he wants you to be full, open, and mean-ingful, catering to his wants as though they were your own. Resistance, resentment, and antipathy are a customer's way of telling you you haven't been helpful. A customer *really* believes he is always right. It's *his* money to keep or spend, not yours.

In this chapter the focus is on how you can improve your commu-nication skills. At the very heart of the communication process are four issues: (1) asking questions, (2) listening, (3) responding to the customer point of view, and (4) handling your emotions. How you react in a give-and-take way with your customer is colored by your

Grid style assumptions. Therefore, each major element of the communication process is examined, style by style, within the Grid framework. To improve your skill in asking questions, for example, diagnose what your "natural" style is of asking questions. Use the 9,9 style as the basis for clues to how you might improve your skill by altering the way you use questions. Repeat the same self-study process with each of the elements.

ASKING QUESTIONS

Where do people get information? There are many sources: books, TV, newspapers, and other communications media. Many of these are not very useful to you as a salesman because they don't contain the kind of information that you want and need to do a good job of moving your product. The kind of information you need is what each customer possesses, uniquely, individually. Your gateway to information is in asking questions to understand his desires, to test the levels of his knowledge, to determine what his expectations are. Questions are the door through which you can pass into the customer's mind to become acquainted with what he is thinking and why he is thinking it.[32]

But posing questions can be a tricky business. If they are good questions you get the kind of information you need and can make a contribution to him. If the questions that are asked are not good, strong, sound questions, they may do a great disservice to you and your efforts to make a sale.

9,1

A typical 9,1 way of asking questions is simply to put forth the query but to neglect explaining to the customer why you seek the information. A 9,1-oriented salesman does this because it's a speedy, direct way to get to the point. He is not wasting his own time nor is he squandering the time of his prospect or customer. As he sees it, the question is necessary and that's sufficient reason for asking it, period.

But let's look at this from the standpoint of the customer. If he doesn't know why you want the information, what does this do to him? Does it make him open and free and spontaneous and expressive? Or does it cause him to go in the opposite direction and be closed, hidden, secluded, and distrustful? It's more likely to do the latter than the former. He doesn't know what the salesman is up to. Not knowing why the information is needed, the customer is likely to feel defensive. It could be that the salesman will misuse the information. It may be that the customer feels you are trying to build a case to use as the basis for corralling him and finally getting him cornered so he can only escape by signing a contract.

Questions can also be asked in a way that soon alerts the customer to the fact that he is being pumped. Just think of the word "pumping" —what does it mean? It means pushing down in order to lift some water from a well. To a customer, this kind of questioning is very suspect. It only reinforces his fear that he is likely to be exploited in other ways too.

1,9

The 1,9 salesman is more inclined to ask questions that the customer might not see as relevant. He asks them in a loose and indirect way. He proceeds in this manner because he wants to avoid saying anything that could be challenged by the customer. His open-ended questions allow a lot of room for the customer to talk and express himself.

But what are the results? The typical customer is very likely to feel that his time is not being used constructively by the salesman acting in this manner. He feels that the conversation is soft, lacking the "brass tacks reality" quality that he may be accustomed to expect. These questions don't warm him toward either the salesman or the product; they cool him off. They don't move him toward a purchase; they move him away.

1,1

A 1,1 salesman is unlikely to formulate and pose questions to his customer. He does not think in terms of what information he, as a salesman, needs in order to provide the customer's problem with a solution. Rather, he is more likely to leave it to the customer to ask questions. He assumes that the customer knows what he needs to know—"if he wants information, he'll ask for it."

5,5

The 5,5-oriented salesman has a preset agenda of questions that are worked out and arranged to move a prospect indirectly toward a positive decision. The strategy is fixed, yet the tactics are flexible. Thus the second, third, and fourth questions may very well be on different subjects. The second question asked is a function of the answer to the first. He selects his third question while displaying great interest in the information the customer has given in answer to his second question, and so on. However, a "prepackaged" quality can quickly be recognized by the customer, who decodes as well as anybody. He realizes that the questions he is being fed are not the kind that help the salesman understand him, but rather are questions that help the salesman maneuver him in a planned direction. As a result, the customer is unlikely to be aroused to enthusiasm by this type of pseudosophisticated, shallow interrogation.

9,9

How would a salesman with a 9,9 orientation go about acquiring the kind of information that is so vital to an effective selling relationship? Prior to asking any questions, he begins by indicating what he knows about the customer's situation, to acquaint the customer with his own degree of understanding. The customer's confidence is increased because he knows now where the salesman stands. Then the salesman asks his questions, letting the customer know *how* it will help him to have the answers he seeks. It takes only a few extra words to answer the customer's implicit Why? beforehand. Also, he might mention that he can do a better job of explaining his product if he can put it in the context that will make it most rewarding and relevant to the customer himself. The salesman, acting in a 9,9 manner, is building a foundation of trust and confidence.

His *manner* of approach communicates several things reinforcing anything he *says*. One thing he is communicating is that he respects the customer as an individual. He does not view him as just another cipher. Other unspoken messages are that he appreciates the customer's ability to think and that the customer's information is valued and will be used during the interview. The questions are not being asked as a gambit to soften him up by getting him to talk. By being open with respect to his own intentions, he is creating in the customer's emotions a readiness to accept him as an honest and genuine salesman and to respond in kind.

Questions versus Interrogation

There's another angle in this questions business. A salesman can make a customer feel weak by asking questions he cannot answer. Whether or not he *should* be able to answer the questions is beside the point. It's what *he* thinks about his inability to answer them that counts. It is possible that he will feel humiliated and resent being given a "test." On the other hand, questions that are meaningful yet relatively easy to answer can enable a person to find enjoyment in giving replies that he knows are right. They build his confidence that he is going to be able to stay in the arena. Even so, questions that are *too* easy run the risk of being viewed by the customer as so trivial that they are wasting his time.

For these reasons, the questions which are posed early in a sales interview should be easy enough for the customer to answer without difficulty. Nevertheless, the more relevant they are, the better. The more difficult questions, which may be vital ones for the customer to consider when approaching a sound purchasing decision, should be introduced later when the salesman has a better understanding of the customer's mind, and conversely. If salesman and customer have come along this far together, it is more likely that later on, if he is asked a tough one which he is unable to answer, the customer will unreservedly say so and not feel incompetent.

Fact versus Evaluation

Another angle on questions is this: the ones that are asked first should be for the purpose of acquiring mainly factual information. Those that are posed later can be more evaluative. The latter are questions that call upon the customer to exercise judgment, to compare and combine facts, and to expose his opinions. There are no quick yes/no answers to them. These are the kinds of questions that are indispensable in sound selling. They aid the salesman in understanding the character of the customer's thinking. This is important in assisting him to come to a sound conclusion. Another aspect of these more thought-provoking questions is that they promote his participation and involvement, providing a more problem-solving orientation during the interview.

Asking questions then is a central feature of good selling. Yet many salesmen seem doubtful about the possible effects of questioning their customers. Perhaps they have not yet come to see what the best possibilities are and how they can be realized. Questions can bind and bond a relationship, rather than bombing it. They can cement a conviction rather than producing a crack-up. They can tie people together rather than tearing them apart. They can forge rather than fracture a closing.

LISTENING AND HEARING

Above all, the sales interview is a conversation. It may have presentation aspects where the salesman does the talking. Yet a good interview is a two-way street—a give-and-take of thoughts and attitudes, of ideas and opinions, of feelings and emotions. It may lead to a meeting of minds and thus to a positive close. But there are many situations in which a detour is taken or the salesman goes down a dead-end street. He does so, not by virtue of any defect in the product or the customer's having no need of it to solve his problem, but rather because of poor listening.

Listening and hearing can be two quite different things. From the point of view of the salesman, he can gain increased acceptance of his ideas through 9,9 Grid listening on the part of the customer and by sound talking. This has already been alluded to in many different ways in this book and elsewhere.[33] What does need deeper analysis is the *salesman's* listening and hearing skills. First, listening does not simply mean being quiet while the customer talks. Second, listening can be biased. What is heard is not necessarily what is said, and this occurs for two reasons. One reason is in the character of talk. The other is in the character of listening. When a person talks, he must find words to express his thoughts and feelings. Words are by no means valid, full statements of what a person is thinking or how he is feeling. Words represent thought and emotions, but they are not "it." They can be poor substitutes. Thoughts are mediated through words and expressed in words.[34] The expression of thoughts can be clear, obscure, or anything in between. Emotions are felt by the speaker as he expresses his thoughts. His words, in themselves, may carry very little indication of these emotions across to the person who hears them, unless the receiver is very attentive to every sign that the speaker displays.

As a result, whenever a person listens to what he is being told, he is reading between the lines. He must piece together, if he can, what is the totality of the speaker's ideas and feelings. He is free to ask questions. Depending on how they are phrased and replied to, these may ensure that his interpretation of what is being said is the intended interpretation that the speaker had in mind to convey. But at a deeper level, the listener's receptivity is a function of his personal nature. No person listens in a completely objective way. It would be impossible to do this. What a person hears may be partly determined by what is said, but it may equally be determined by what is inside the listener. The message that comes in gets mixed in with a mass of experience, emotions, and attitudes and gets its coloration from what has gone on and is going on in the listener's own experience.[35] To the degree that the listener is able to sort out and keep separate his own opinions from what is really being said, he is listening attentively.

The importance of all this is that selling is as much listening as it is talking. To listen accurately, the salesman must seek the melody, not just the tone. He must grasp the meaning, not just the words. He must analyze the intention of the speaker, not just his language. When he does this, he is far more likely to make an effective presentation, deal soundly with objections, place true meaning on apparently irrelevant remarks, and give sound answers to questions.

9,1

9,1 listening is defensive listening. What is it that the customer is saying which is a threat to effective closing? If the salesman can locate in what the customer is saying, thinking, and feeling, that which may prevent him from buying, he can then launch an attack on those points and win a sale by disposing of them quickly. As a result, defensive listening has its advantages. It does keep the salesman alert to the opinions, thoughts, and attitudes being revealed which, if not understood, could lead to difficulty. The disadvantage is that his listening may not be at all perceptive. What he hears stimulates the sensitiveness in him and is likely to trigger his own aggressive attitude. Poor listening can convert a customer's emotionally neutral question into a strong objection—as the salesman hears it. He then tries to shoot the "objection" down, and the customer, not wanting to be humiliated, begins to feel emotions of resistance in himself. Once aroused, they may in fact turn his initial query into a criticism and a win-lose battle begins. The ensuing fight may be stimulating, but it is stimulating to the glands, respiration, and pulse rate, not to sales volume.

1,9

1,9 listening narrows reception in a different way. It is not defensive listening. Rather, the feature most characteristic of 1,9 listening is that the salesman hears what he wants to hear. He adds to it what he would like to have heard instead. He is sensitive to the emotions in the situation and interprets the message differently depending on whether he senses hostility or friendliness, acceptance or rejection. This is particularly so in the case of objections; he does not like to hear them; they are unpleasant and disconcerting—"surely he doesn't mean that?" So he is not listening for understanding. Therefore his answers are likely to be off beam, responding to the emotion rather than focusing on a sound resolution of the objection. Listening for what he wants to hear, though, has some advantages. He can sometimes supplement an approving remark made by the customer about the product, with a series of additional points of information, all of which further a positive attitude on the part of the customer. But despite this, the customer is unlikely to find much gratification in the sales discussion. When he poses questions or raises objections, the answers he receives have a bland, insipid quality. The customer seeks food for thought; the salesman gives him tranquilizers.

1,1

1,1 listening is likely to be very inattentive. This salesman is neither emotionally involved with his product or himself, nor is he enamored with his own sales technique. Thus, he will provide ample opportunity for the customer to talk, but the salesman tunes himself out and thinks about other things. When he fails to hear a positive indication of customer readiness to buy, or senses resistance, he begins to close down the store mentally and says to himself, "Well, this one's gone down the drain—there's nothing more to discuss." In other words, his listening mistake is that of short-circuiting the entire sales interview rather than moving forward in a sound manner.

5,5

A person listening in a 5,5 way is attempting to pigeonhole each remark he hears according to some preestablished system of interpretation. If he can fit what is being said into a particular category, he then knows what answer to give. He may think, "Ah, he's *Interested*. Now I can start building his *Confidence*," and go on to phrase his reply in this direction of persuasion. This kind of listening can lead to hearing that is good to the extent that the preestablished framework is good. The major difficulty with it is that no frame of reference can be so refined as to catalog all the nuances of thought-plus-feelings that characterize the expressions of customers. Each is unique; all are different. The Grid system is certainly not intended to substitute for interpretive thinking—it does not indicate "automatic" responses to particular customer styles as soon as these are recognized. Yet a 5,5-oriented salesman might try to mechanize it in this way. Thus, the 5,5 restricted scope of listening is likely to lead to answers that, while they may be relevant, are not completely on target.

9,9

The prime ingredient of 9,9 listening is the salesman's knowledge that the essence of thought and feeling is never captured in words. He knows that words are less than perfect tools of communication and that he needs to understand genuinely what the question, reservation, or objection by the customer truly means within the context of the other person's nature and circumstances. For this reason, the 9,9-oriented salesman would be more likely to repeat, not in the same words as they were spoken but according to his understanding of those words, the question or inquiry made by the customer, so as to verify it. In this way he can assure himself that he genuinely understands, to the fullest extent possible, what the customer had in his mind when he spoke. By doing this the 9,9-oriented salesman is in the best practical position to be able to answer whatever it is that he has heard, according to the needs of the speaker, and so provide him a satisfactory answer. He summarizes frequently to ensure that he and the customer are on the same wavelength.

But the receptivity aspect of the 9,9 listening emerges from the salesman's personal disposition. He is unlikely to screen or distort what is being said by mingling his own views with the customer's in such a way as to misinterpret or attach false emphases to what the other person is saying. He is able to keep his own feelings separate, so that they do not affect his capacity to hear.

RESPONDING TO THE CUSTOMER POINT OF VIEW

To a salesman, it might appear that the "dream" interview would be one in which he led the conversation and the customer compliantly listened, becoming ever more favorably disposed toward purchasing. Suddenly, unable to control his excitement, the customer bursts out with, "Yes, you've convinced me, and I'll sign the order form right now." One can tolerate this kind of interruption, whatever one's opinion of the other kinds.

From the standpoint of the customer, though, this is not a scenario that he is likely to follow. A sales presentation, no matter how smoothly it flows, can never correspond exactly to the path of development in a person's mind, of understanding and readiness to buy. There are many possible thoughts and emotions that can occur to a customer as he listens. He feels like commenting and does. His remarks, which break the continuity of the salesman's discourse, may come at any time. Some of them may be directly relevant to what is being said at that time, but the salesman doesn't see the connection. Others are in the nature of general objections to what he, the salesman, is presenting.

Interruptions in a conversation need to be studied because they are indications that the customer's point of view is at variance with the salesman's presentation. The topic in this section is one which is distinct from the very difficult problem (which was mentioned earlier) of dealing constructively and positively with objections. *How about interruptions which are not objections?*

This analysis, then, is of interruptions (but not objections) by the customer while the salesman is speaking. You can also reverse its terms and recognize that his feelings when you interrupt him may be very much the same as your feelings when he interrupts you.

9,1

Let's look at the pattern of a 9,1-oriented salesman rather than at any specific interruption. He reacts with impatience; an interruption slows down his presentation. Many times he sees interruptions as irrelevant and therefore not worthy of being dealt with. In either event, they are likely to be ignored or, with a figurative swing of the arm, simply brushed aside.

How does a customer, who is trying to state his point of view, respond to this treatment? He is likely to feel rejected, resentful, and resistant. What appears to be irrelevant to the salesman is likely to be highly relevant to the customer. Its relevance may not be to the sale but to the customer's desire for the salesman to understand him or to hear what he has on his mind. For example, he may recently have had problems, and he simply wants to use a period in the sales interview to blow off steam. If the salesman doesn't let him release the pressure, it remains pent up. He may be turning the problem over in his mind rather than listening to the presentation. Or he may want to tell the salesman about something that has made him proud and excited, for example, that he has just been promoted or that his son has been graduated from college. Or it may be a dramatic experience that he had during a vacation or business trip. This kind of interruption has no relevance to the subject of the sales interview. The fact that the customer is giving the information indicates that he classes the salesman as a person who, until proved otherwise, does not consider him a nonentity. Thus, being ignored or brushed aside will probably raise barriers in his mind against the salesman and, by extension, the product he is attempting to sell.

1,9

A 1,9 way of dealing with the same kind of interruptions is to treat them with the utmost appreciation and respect. The salesman sincerely wishes to avoid giving the customer any indication whatsoever that he is not valued as a person. At the same time, the positive tone of the interruptions reduces his own anxiety, based on fear of being rejected. So he responds warmly. The subject matter of the interruption is put in the forefront, to be fully discussed, while the content of the sales interview is set aside indefinitely.

But what are the results? There are likely to be several. One is that the interview stretches out to an indeterminable length. It wanders and meanders all over the place, having little crispness and less direction. One topic of the free-flowing conversation stimulates another and so on. The closing recedes ever further beyond the horizon. The sales interview finally is closed, but the sale is not. The customer runs out of time. He has not gathered enough information to enable him to see how the product could solve his problem. Unless he himself is 1,9, he is likely to realize that this kind of meandering and wandering is wasteful. He thinks of what he could have done had he not been distracted. So although the 1,9-oriented salesman's intention is to create liking and respect—an atmosphere in which a purchase may be made—he employs methods that tend to be self-defeating.

1,1

When a 1,1-oriented salesman is interrupted, he may take this as a sign that the customer is uninterested in buying and wants to steer him off the subject so as to conclude the interview. His response to this is to assume that all is lost and to start thinking of what to do with his free time. "That one didn't take long; maybe I can shop for my new fishing rod before going to the 11:30 appointment uptown." While dealing perfunctorily with the interruption, he is mentally buttoning his coat and closing his briefcase. He is not listening to the customer and discussing the matter with him so as to give and take what he can, before resuming the sales interview. He has already done a mental walkout. Maybe the customer was trying to make a relevant comment about his situation and the use of the product, but this salesman will never know. By giving up, he fulfills his own prophecy and walks away from a potential sale.

5,5

The 5,5 way of treating interruptions is to appreciate that customers often are disposed to talk about matters that are not directly relevant to the sales interview. One must humor them. It is frequently possible to move them to a purchase decision via their own individual byways. So the salesman accepts the interruption as a detour through which the sales interview must pass in order to get to a closing. Thus, the interruption is acknowledged by a courteous pause. He listens to whatever is said and tries to connect it with part of his preestablished sales presentation. If no connection seems possible, he hears the customer out, makes some bland remark as, "That's very interesting," and shifts back to the main road.

9,9

A 9,9-oriented salesman understands and respects human relationships and appreciates that life is more than logic. Life should be guided by logic, but life is felt through emotions. While his basic motivations relate to helping the customer constructively to find solutions to his problems, his deeper appreciation of customers is that they, like himself, have needs and emotions and feelings and frustrations. All of these may pull conversations away from the straight paths of logic. He does not see such departures from the shortest path as unnecessary detours, but rather as part of the complexity of living individuals.

Whatever the reason for the customer's interruption, a 9,9 salesman has respect for his feelings. The interruption may not seem to bring out any new and important information bearing on the subject of the sales interview, but it certainly is important from the customer's standpoint. So the salesman feels that it is important for him to understand what it is that the customer is saying and why he interrupted at that point. Taking this kind of diagnostic attitude, the salesman is in a sound position to appreciate the customer as a person by comprehending how he thinks, what he thinks about, and why. Much of this analytical information is of background value in aiding the salesman in seeing how he might present his product so as to make it most understandable to the customer. He realizes that every customer is unique and that no two persons have exactly the same patterns of thought, that every person is distinctive and unique in his own experience and emotions.

In any event, a 9,9-oriented salesman would not attempt to insist that the customer must always remain on the subject. To be irritated at apparently aimless meandering and by disconnected statements which seem to have no bearing on the topic of discussion is only to lose the deeper possibilities that a sales conversation presents. To understand why the interruption can be a key to gaining and holding a customer's attention, consider what a sound handling of it can do for him. It tells him that his thoughts, ideas, opinions, and feelings are acknowledged as just as important as the salesman's own in the discussion that precedes his decision whether to purchase or not.

DEALING WITH EMOTIONS

If life were all logic, the biggest barrier to human effectiveness wouldn't appear. But rationality is not the strongest theme in human affairs. It is logic that gets solutions to problems and gets things done; but emotions supply the power. They are the engine. They are the wellspring. They are the cause of action.

How emotions influence the customer behavior in a sales interview has been discussed up to this point. Now attention is turned to emotions as you find them in yourself, and what you can do, constructively, in living with your emotions. It may very well be that when a man understands his own emotions, he is in a much better position to be helpful in dealing with others who are being driven every which way by engines of emotion rather than guiding themselves steadily through reasoning and logic.

Where do emotions come from? Why do people have them?

Emotions are in evidence in the higher and lower forms of life. They are present in animals as well as in men. They serve a purpose.

Negative emotions arise as signals to a person that things are not right, that danger lies ahead, that risk to life and limb may be in the offing. In modern society, these life and limb risks are not as great as once they were, of course, but risks to one's sense of well-being are probably greater now than in former times. Though the circumstances of living have changed, every person still has deep reservoirs of emotions. The complex social environment today has more than enough stimulation to provoke many of the most negative of human emotions as responses to threats to well-being. On the positive side, there are emotions of love and enjoyment of one's job and of excitement in performing it well. What do these come from? How can they be understood? The positive emotions arise when a person feels secure, successful, and effective. They come forth when he is able to master the situations that confront him and to build confidence in his capacity to deal with the problems in his life.

If your emotions are out of tune with the situation, they undoubtedly will get in the way of your establishing a sound relationship with a customer. This is why it's important to look deeply into the whole matter of emotions and feelings.

9,1

A 9,1-oriented person views emotions as a source of weakness. A person should keep a stiff upper lip and never show his emotions. Men don't let them get in the way of their action. So, it might be said that a person acting from 9,1 assumptions has learned to deny and disregard his own feelings—or at least, the "sentimental" range within the spectrum. He may have suppressed them and pushed them down so deeply into himself that he doesn't recognize that they are there. His disregard for people may slip through in his use of humor—it is hard-hitting and carries a sting for those who are its targets. He may discharge them by having intense prejudices and hates, such as against minority groups or certain ideologies in politics or religion, which provide a channel for release. He has negative emotions, but he doesn't experience them for what they really are. Rather he takes them out on society by his own righteous indignation, all the while denying he has any emotions at all. Only when he can't control situations are his emotions likely to break through and become apparent. Then his temper flares, and under exceptional circumstances it becomes a fit of rage.

A person who controls his emotions in these ways, though there are other 9,1 ways, too, may seem to be efficient. All is business: no play, no interruptions, no irrelevancies, get to the point, drive hard, move in, close the deal, get out. What gets lost is the richness of understanding, human sympathy, and the ability to feel how the other person feels. Furthermore, controlling negative emotions in this way often results in an inability to enjoy the positive ones. Success is not gratifying, achievement not rewarding; life affords few pleasures.

If a salesman happens to lean in a 9,1 direction, he may be able to notice that these characteristics of emotions, as described above, resemble his own approach. It can be most important for him to look inward. If he finds he has these emotional tendencies, he may also find that they are more likely to impede successful selling. What can he do about it?

Every person can learn to be more open with himself and to recognize what it is that he is doing, or not doing, which is producing the consequences that can be observed. If a 9,1-oriented person finds that he has a self-canceling way of dealing with his own emotions, a good place to start in doing something about it is with his temper. It is most likely to be damaging to customer relations. He can look at situations that get his dander up. What is it in those situations that makes him feel weak and threatened so that he reacts with temper against the threat that he feels from them? If he reacts in this way, he can then ask, Do I deal with these situations better by unloading anger or is there a different approach that might be far more constructive for myself? Most people, when they examine the situation that results in outbursts of temper, find that this way of reacting works *against* their best interests rather than for them. By seeing more clearly what the features are in situations that cause his temper to flare, a person then can become insightful and intelligent about how to deal with the problem itself, rather than responding with a blowup. If he develops personal insight in this way, he is likely to find that he is more able to deal with others in a relaxed yet vigorous manner, with all the gains of better listening, clearer logic, and more enjoyment.

1,9

1,9 ways of adjusting to emotion are where the accent is on the positive and enjoyment comes not during action or with achievement, but in togetherness. This means turning away from situations that arouse anxiety or that could lead to the person's feeling he might be rejected by others. Warmth and affection are emotions with which 1,9-oriented people feel quite secure. They are the very feelings that a 9,1-oriented person feels to be sticky, at least during working hours. The emotions that a 1,9-oriented person feels uncomfortable with are antipathy and antagonism. He is attracted toward situations which produce harmony and good feelings and runs away from situations that might have tension or conflict in them.

Some of these 1,9 emotional dispositions can be helpful in promoting sales, but backing off from the anxiety components in human relationships can be a great hindrance. These are the kinds of emotions that make it difficult for a person to deal with objections and to respond validly to complaints. Yet it is in dealing with objections, interruptions, complaints, and questions that so much conviction building is done.

What can a person who leans in a 1,9 direction do to strengthen himself? He can make clear to himself the characteristics of those situations that make him feel apprehensive. Why is it that he turns off his hearing aid and wants to escape from situations that promote anxiety? If the properties of situations that make him feel this way are clear to him, he can then discipline himself to stay in such situations longer than he formerly did and to see whether or not they, in fact, will be painful to him. His experiment in living with the more negative and hostile emotions can give him insight into how he can be more comfortable and constructive in responding to them rather than attempting to escape from them.

1,1

The 1,1 orientation to emotions is almost a contradiction in terms. A person who has gravitated into 1,1 attitudes has disconnected his emotions from circumstances at hand. He does not have the interest he may formerly have had in steering clear of risky situations or venturing into new situations that might be emotionally invigorating.

A person who is adjusting to emotional situations in a 1,1 way *can* do something about it. The key is this: it has been learned that many people who have adjusted to a 1,1 attitude aren't aware that they have slumped over into a kind of emotional slumber. How people go to sleep emotionally is not too difficult to understand either. Many a person has become 1,1 about the emotions and involvements of his job, yet remains highly involved, committed, and challenged by community interests, hobbies, and home. Once the person who has gone to emotional sleep on his job comes to see how inconsistent this aspect of behavior is and what he is missing, he can awaken himself, sometimes with a sense of rediscovery. Yet it is not easy for a person to reach this point of self-awareness. The best way perhaps is for him to run a check on his involvements and enthusiasms in comparison with those of other salesmen or other people he knows. He can ask himself the question, Are they overenthusiastic or am I underenthusiastic? Frequently he will find himself concluding that it is not they who are overenthusiastic. It only looks that way by virtue of the fact that he has lost his own enthusiasm. A perceptible gap between the emotions he feels toward a situation and the emotions others feel toward the same kind of situation is a clue that he has begun to gravitate into 1,1 ways.

5,5

A 5,5-oriented salesman has his own distinctive emotional disposition. A way of picturing him is that he avoids the intense emotions of anger, hate, and antipathy by not pushing himself as hard as the 9,1 person. He does not slide into the soft indulging emotions so much enjoyed by 1,9 people. Neither does he drift into uninvolvement in the 1,1 way. By positioning himself safely, he avoids getting out on an emotional limb where anybody could cut him off. This mode of emotional adjustment is conservative. It is sheltered from risk, but what it does is to cut him off from the richness of living too. It makes him seem mechanical and feel emotionally shallow. This shows through in the sense that he appears to calibrate his emotions almost as an engineer might set the controls of a machine to carry out some process.

To "fit the situation" he responds as he is expected to rather than as he feels.

What can a person whose emotional adjustment is of the 5,5 variety do about it? What he can do is stretch himself. He has more potential flexibility and emotional range than he is using. He needs to undertake an emotional building program. He can do this by letting himself be challenged in hostile situations, by allowing himself to relax and be genuine in situations that are positive, warm, and friendly. By deepening his interest and letting himself go, he can feel the enthusiasm of being spontaneous and more actively involved in the events going on around him.

9,9

The 9,9 approach to emotions is different .from any of those described above. First of all, 9,9 emotions are genuine. They are valid responses to situations that are being viewed from an objective orientation. A 9,9 person can experience emotions of antipathy toward those responsible for injustice. He can feel emotions of affection for those capable of responding with affection. He can feel the plight of people who are uninvolved and withdrawn, and he can comprehend with understanding the conservative, emotional, "playing it safe" attitudes of the man whose emotions are always in the middle. He can challenge situations that are wrong and acknowledge situations that are right, because he has learned that his emotions are a trustworthy source of self-judgment. They provide a basis of self-confidence for coping constructively with situations across the whole spectrum of his encounters.

People who can handle their emotions in a 9,9 way, once they have a fuller and deeper understanding of this orientation, often are able to enrich further their capacities for strong and yet sound emotional response. One of the key ways is by helping others to be more comfortable through responding in 9,9 ways themselves toward situations that provoke emotional states. For example, he can say to a person who is up in arms in a 9,1 temper reaction, "Hey, let's cool it. Let's sit down and discuss this situation and what is causing the difficulties we have." His cool-headedness and constructive approach help to bring the logic of reality back into focus for the person who has lost control of his emotions. With a person whose emotions are of a 1,9 variety, he can help him experiment in staying with situations that have more conflict and hostility in them, giving the 1,9 person support where he feels threatened and encouragement while he is learning. He can challenge the person whose emotions are of the 1,1 kind to look at himself more clearly and to answer for himself whether or not he has taken a wrong exit. With a 5,5 person, he can do much the same as with 1,9, helping the 5,5 person to venture into deeper commitment, to cope with the strongest currents that may be flowing beneath the surface of a situation. In doing each of these things, a 9,9-oriented person is enriching his own emotional strength and gaining insights that can aid him in becoming even stronger and more effective himself.

The most important thing that a 9,9 person can do is apply his skill in facing up to situations that have conflict in them. This consists of bringing the emotions that are being expressed into line with the objective requirements of the situation in a sound manner by critiquing what in his own behavior may be creating barriers and by inviting others to critique him in order to gain insight into himself.

So we have the fact that life has deep emotional undercurrents. These emotional undercurrents are not well understood by people. But they can become more *understandable* by people. A person doesn't gain much help from another who simply tells him to act naturally or "be yourself." He can get help and strength from others through the readiness to let himself be challenged and to challenge others, to critique, and, most importantly, to listen to the feedback which is widely available to him if he will turn *on* nature's hearing aid to learn what others are prepared to say and what he needs to know.

But even here an incorrect conclusion might be drawn if you interpret what is being said as suggesting, "Where there's a will there's a way," that if a person simply wills himself to self-improvement, self-improvement will result. This is not necessarily true.

What does seem to be true is that much personal learning of the self-improvement variety can arise from having an attitude of willingness to learn. However, the capacity for an individual to learn about himself can be greatly extended. Ways in which you can use Grid theory to improve your selling effectiveness are in the next chapter.

chapter thirteen

Self-development

You EXAMINED YOURSELF in the Grid mirror while reading Chapter 2. What you saw at that time can now be analyzed. Even better, you may want to reexamine the description of yourself you made then and to correct it now that you have a more thorough understanding of the Grid in your own salesmanship.[36]

REEXAMINING YOUR GRID STYLE

How did you see yourself? Did you come out as predominantly 9,9? Or was it 9,1; 1,9; 1,1; or 5,5? If what you saw was 9,9, is that the real you?

This question can be answered by examining empirical data. Men with sales experience have looked at themselves in the Grid mirror just as you did in Chapter 2. Then they attended a Grid Seminar where there were many activities and two significant outcomes. One involved a deeper study of the Grid by each participant who tested his own knowledge of it against the understanding of other participants as well as against objective criteria. He learned the Grid in this deeper way. Each participant then got feedback from his colleagues concerning the dominant Grid style they had observed in him during the week's discussions and problem-solving activities. Then he reexamined himself in the Grid mirror again and described what he saw to be his own dominant and backup Grid styles.

As you can see in Box 5, a large shift in self-assessment, particularly with respect to the 9,9 Grid style, occurred between the first time of looking in the Grid mirror and the second. Prior to their seminars, 83 percent saw themselves as 9,9 in the Grid mirror. After the Grid Seminar was completed and when they looked in the mirror again, 33 percent saw themselves as 9,9.

How can this reduction of 50 percent be accounted for? There are several explanations:

1. *Better understanding:* a more thorough comprehension of the concepts makes it possible to be more objective. You can't see as well in a foggy mirror.

2. *Self-deception:* when a person looks inside himself, he is likely to make a misjudgment of what he finds there. He looks at his intentions. Most people have good intentions that correspond generally with a 9,9 orientation, but the individual is unlikely to see his own behavior which may be, and often is, contradictory to his good intentions.

3. *New data:* when people receive feedback as to how others see their behavior, they may learn things about themselves which they previously had not recognized. With this new information, they can see themselves more objectively.

So, based on these data, this chapter on development is written from the point of view that only one in three readers is likely to be truly 9,9.

But the next question is, What do people want to be?

This question also can be answered by empirical data which were gathered in the following way. After completing Grid Seminars, many thousands of participants have answered this question by examining personal values as well as cultural practices, indicating what the "soundest" Grid style is, the most effective backup, and the next. Their evaluations are shown in Box 5. Almost universally, 9,9 is endorsed as the best Grid style, 9,1 and 5,5 tie for second place, and 1,9 and 1,1 are last in order.

BOX 5 Reactions of Grid Seminar Participants to the 9,9 Grid Style

Percent Responding	What Is Your Grid Style?		What Is the "Best" Grid Style for Sound Human Relationships?
	Before Grid Seminars	After Grid Seminars	

The implication from the data presented in Box 5 is that many participants deceive themselves into believing they are 9,9, but under close self-scrutiny, the majority are not conducting their human relationships in that way. Yet, the second implication is that almost everyone thinks this would be the best way to conduct his professional human relationships.

From Box 5 we know what salesmen think the soundest sales strategy to be. This can be tested against sales results that are obtained in actual sales situations when real life is being studied under experimental conditions. These selling experiments include a four-sequence activity. Participants acting as customers buy from salesmen selling different brands of the same products. The experiment is designed so that a customer chooses one of two competing salesmen to do business with. Then comes a double diagnosis. Salesmen identify customer

Grid styles, customers identify salesmen styles. The activity ends with a critique session. Successes or failures of salesmen are analyzed. A second selling experiment takes place the next day. Yesterday's salesmen become today's customers and vice-versa. Summaries of results and the data that are gathered highlight the ingredients of success.

The data obtained permit measurement of the effectiveness of each of the Sales Grid styles. As shown in Box 6, based on data from 136

BOX 6   Sales Success by Grid Styles

Grid Styles	Percent of Sales Made by Grid Style
9,9	61.0
5,5	23.5
9,1	8.1
1,9	6.6
1,1	0.8

participants in both public and in-company seminars, 61 percent of the successful sales were made by salesmen seen by their customers as 9,9. The next most effective style was 5,5. Where one of the two competing salesmen is seen as 9,9 and the other is not, 9,9 makes the sale in 94 percent of the instances. This suggests that other styles are rejected when they are compared with solution selling.

PROPERTIES OF A 9,9-ORIENTED SALESMAN

Before dealing with the issue of how people might change, it will be useful to review the major properties of 9,9 as a Sales Grid style.

The viewpoint of a 9,9-oriented salesman is that when a customer is considering a purchase proposition, he has his own or a company problem to solve. This problem is one of defining *what* is wanted and of relating these wants to the *means* by which they can be satisfied. "What" includes intangible, subjective factors as well as material objects. "Means" includes financial as well as product considerations. Because of the changing nature of most of these variables, the *total customer problem is unique at the time each sales interview takes place*. It is unique not only for sales interviews with different customers, but also for successive interviews with the same customer. A 9,9-oriented salesman is committed to selling solutions to his customers' problems. For these reasons, he:

1. Has expert knowledge of his product
2. Gains an in-depth knowledge of his customer
3. Keeps well informed of competitor's products and strategies
4. Is ready to compare competitor's products objectively with his own
5. Helps the customer to make a reasoned purchasing decision
6. Gains the customer's active participation and involvement in the sales interview
7. Sees the customer's thoughts and emotions as of a whole cloth needing to be integrated within the sales interview
8. Tries to identify underlying reasons when conflict arises and to work them through to common understanding
9. Samples and tests the customer's knowledge during the opening to assess where to begin and where to correct any misunderstanding he may have
10. Conducts the interview as a problem-solving discussion
11. Creates opportunities for the customer to express and discuss objections early and throughout the interview
12. Summarizes the discussion as the basis for moving toward a close
13. Shows a strong interest in understanding the customer's reasons when the closing is unsuccessful
14. Keeps in sound contact with established accounts
15. Treats the prompt and positive handling of complaints as of utmost importance in maintaining an account
16. Deals with rush business in a flexible but customer-satisfying way
17. Keeps personal integrity constantly in the forefront through openness and candor by providing facts, data, and logic and by creating valid expectations
18. Plans and schedules activities in terms of sales objectives
19. Prospects by treating every customer as a gatekeeper and by continuously analyzing market characteristics and potential
20. Sees that service commitments are met with top-grade service provided
21. Controls his expenses to get full value in terms of sales results from the money he spends

22. Critiques himself to find the causes of his failures as well as of his successes

23. Uses the profit logic of a private enterprise society to guide his selling actions

24. Gives help, which is over and above the business requirements of his sales contacts, in a free and spontaneous way

Thirty years ago people often said, "Life begins at forty." But in this era you're over the hill at thirty, according to the "now" generation. What they mean is that most people have become complacent, stuck in their ruts, and, as a consequence, unable to change after reaching thirty. Whether life begins at forty or stops at thirty has nothing to do with bones, muscles, nerves, and blood. It has everything to do with a man's point of view. He can get crusty and dead from the neck up at twenty or he can be lively, brisk, frisky, and growing professionally at fifty.

COMPARISON LEARNING

Learning is essential for change, so we need to know more about conditions that are favorable for learning how to change.

Conditions are favorable for learning whenever a man can make comparisons between two or more things. Then he can see similarities and differences, analyze the reasons for them, and determine which of the two is better in terms of relative merit. When he sees similarities and differences, understands the reasons beneath the surface, and can evaluate them on a "degrees of good and bad" basis, he is in a position to plot a course of action for how to get from where he was to where he wants to be.

Now let's take this concept of how learning occurs and apply it to changing your Grid style if that's what you want to do, or strengthening the one you have if that's the conclusion you have reached. First of all, the Grid itself provides the basis for a series of comparisons. In many different ways, as you have read this book, you have been comparing 9,9 with 9,1 with 5,5 with 1,9 with 1,1. You can see the similarities between 9,1 and 9,9. One is that both have a high concern for making a sale. 9,1 disregards the customer as the unique and distinctive individual, while 9,9 appreciates the individual as the person for whom the salesman should have the utmost respect. That's the key difference.

1,9 and 1,1 also are similar. Neither of them has much concern for making a sale, but a salesman with a 1,9 attitude enjoys people whereas the 1,1-oriented salesman is indifferent to them. So you can see similarities and differences here too. A 5,5-oriented salesman, in comparison with all others, shares some similarities but very important differences. In some respects, he is in the direction of 9,9, but the major difference is that his approach is shallow and mechanical rather than deep and committed. So here is the fundamental basis for comparison.

Comparison of Grid Positions

A first step in strengthening yourself is to be as clear as crystal about the concepts of the Grid. You can test yourself. Here's how. Take some particular selling situation that you now have. Write down what the 9,1 attitude toward that selling situation would be. Then move over and describe the 1,9 attitude. What would be the 1,1 reaction? How would a 5,5-oriented salesman think about that situation? Finally, picture the 9,9 approach to dealing with it.

Taking your own statements, you might then want to switch back to parts of this book which are related to the same or similar selling situations and test your statements against the text. You might want to change some and refine others. You will find that writing statements in this way will aid you in diagnosing various ways of seeing a selling situation and therefore of dealing with it. If you will do this from time to time, you will find that it continues strengthening your understanding of the Grid. It will help you in self-diagnosis, because you will be able to see ways of dealing with the situation that might differ from your presently characteristic approach to it.

Compare Your Attitudes with the Grid

You can compare and analyze similarities and differences among these five major orientations, but, of course, there is something far more important if you want to change or strengthen yourself. It is to compare your own attitudes with those of the Grid and see which Grid orientation corresponds with your own. This involves searching for similarities between you and each of the five positions. This will tell you where you are. A second step is to come to your own conclusions as to why you are there and then decide whether being *there* is where you want to be. In coming to this conclusion, it is helpful to analyze which of the Grid styles is not at all like you. This is important because it will tell you something about your aversions. Once you understand what it is you dislike, you very well may want to ask yourself if you act poorly with customers who represent in their Grid styles the Grid style you reject in yourself. This will help you see what it is about some customers that bugs you, and you can answer questions for yourself as to how you might work more effectively with customers who represent the things you dislike in yourself. The chances are that once you understand your own feelings and actions, you will find it possible to be more constructive and positive in working with your customers.

Choosing What Is Ideal for You

But there is another way you can use the Grid as the basis for self-development. It involves identifying the Grid style that fits you the best. This is the one that you think would be ideal as the most effective way of selling. Go even further: identify what is the soundest backup for you to adopt and what situations would impel you to use it. Knowing the Grid description that currently fits you best—as you have been operating—and knowing the Grid style that *would* be best in terms of effectiveness provide the basis for you to set development objectives for yourself. In making this comparison between the *actual* you and the *ideal* you, you will be able to see what it is you do that is sound and what it is you do that is not. You will also be able to see what it is you *do not do* that you would need to do if you were to act in a truly sound way.

Let's assume that you selected 9,9 as the ideal. That's the most likely possibility. No matter how sound any particular Grid style you chose might seem to be, it is realistic only insofar as it is workable. 9,9 is a practical and very sound orientation and problem-solving approach which you are probably capable of adopting and to which most customers can respond favorably. However, there are situations where 9,9—or any style you adopt as the soundest—may be unworkable. Your skill in selling under this approach may be insufficient. In a particular interview, the behavior of your customer may be such as to obstruct completely your chosen approach. Your soundest selling style may be unworkable because of certain characteristics of your product or because of some of your organization's policies and practices. In situations such as these, you have no choice but to move into a backup strategy until you see an opportunity to return to the dominant style that you have found to be generally the soundest.

The real test in self-development is learning to increase the skill and flexibility with which 9,9 solutions can be implemented, so that it will seldom be necessary to adopt backup assumptions. You may also be able to find ways of initiating and taking part in constructive discussion and improvement of your company's product and its marketing strategies.

Compare Your Selling Strategies with Other Salesmen's

Let's move into another basis for comparison for a moment and see what else you can do for your own self-development. In many situations there are other salesmen, either ones with whom you compete or colleagues of yours who are selling the same products. Use the Grid to analyze them in your own mind. What are their strengths and weaknesses; what Grid styles do you see in those who are least effective; what conclusion does this lead you to? Can you see behavior in those who are most effective which is different from your own and which, if you were to adopt it, would give you even more strength? Do you see behavior in the least effective salesman which you see in yourself— behavior that you need to change? There is another thing you can do here by reversing the mirror. Give this book to your boss or to salesman colleagues, that is, to people who have had a chance to observe you being governed by your present attitudes toward selling. Perhaps they have even watched you perform in sales situations. Get them to read it, inviting them to read *you* somewhere in its pages, and to jot down notes where they would put you on the Grid. Then, when they have done this, sit down and let them give you their feedback on your Grid style. This is an excellent basis for comparison because you can then evaluate what they think of you against what you think of yourself. This kind of comparison is particularly important because it gives you another person's point of view; it gets you outside of your own skin.

Ask Your Wife

You can also do this kind of data gathering about yourself by giving this book to your wife. She undoubtedly knows you as well and perhaps better than anyone else. She knows what turns you on and what turns you off, what you accept and what you can't take. If you ask her to read the book and then return to Chapter 2 and pick out paragraphs and elements that are most typical of you, you can gain a great deal of good understanding of yourself through her eyes. Incidentally, if you do this, you may find that it has some very good effects on your marriage. Many people have found the Grid a useful way of analyzing how husband and wife exert influence on one another and also how both act with regard to children. This can be very important to you beyond your interest in selling.

Compare One Customer with Another

You have another basis for comparison when you constantly study and compare one customer with another. In this way you get to know your customers in Grid terms so that you can see what it is in them that increases or reduces your own effectiveness. When you see this clearly, you are in a position to work more effectively with the customer's Grid style.

In conclusion, you will be well rewarded by comparing, analyzing, evaluating, and drawing conclusions as these relate to what you should or should not do as a basis for your next step in development. This is a truly sound basis for self-development.

Experiment with and Critique Your Selling Styles

Although making comparisons, drawing conclusions, and setting personal objectives is necessary, it is not enough. There is a good reason why. It is that you have to act upon your self-recommendations and then study the consequences. Did your actions do what you planned to do? Did they produce good or bad results? Why? More learning seems to come from critiquing yourself, but you can only critique yourself if you experiment. Design personal experiments that you can carry out; conduct an experiment, evaluate it, and plan next steps.

A good way of doing this is to design an experiment so that it too will provide a basis for comparison. Take, for example, two comparable selling situations. Apply your characteristic way in one of them; this is your control condition. Apply your new strategy in the other; this is your experimental condition. Having conducted the experiment, study the results from each. Did the experimental condition produce better or poorer results than the control condition? Why? What is the implication? Was it a poor experiment? Was it a good experiment you had difficulty in carrying out? Was it a good experiment that failed to give the results you expected? When you can answer these questions, you are in a position to repeat the experiment in order to develop skill in doing the new action in comparison with the old, or perhaps in retaining the old practice while combining it with others. Then you can design additional experiments.

Just one word of caution. Think the experiment through well. Do one at a time. Be thorough. Continue treating customers *as* customers, not as laboratory monkeys.

Develop and Strengthen Your Resilience

Over a period of a day or a week you conduct a number of sales interviews. You are meeting with prospects whom you think to be potential customers. You open and go through your presentation with enthusiasm. You do your best to involve the customer and to bring him to a purchase decision that will give him lasting satisfaction. He turns you down. You go to your next appointment. Again you do your best, but no sale results. You check over what you have been doing and how each customer has responded to you. You can't find any flaw in your approach. It was achieving sales results until very recently. You make your next call and again emerge with no sale. Is it just one of those days or are you going stale? Is it a bum territory or are you the bum in the territory? Thoughts like these are revolving in your mind, with awareness of the amount of commission you could have made but didn't. How do you feel now as you go to your next sales interview appointment after three, four, or more successive knockbacks?

What do you do? Watch yourself carefully, for here is a point at which some salesmen take an emotional nosedive. They ensure by their own actions that the first few unproductive interviews are followed by a long sequence of resultless meetings with customers. They are all churned up, classifying themselves as losers, feeling doomed. These emotions can have many negative effects, often in combination. Although the next prospect has neither knowledge of nor collusion with any of the previous interviewees, the salesman may go in to him convinced that he's got to sell harder than ever before and win this one if it's the last thing he ever does. He switches to a backup which most likely is far more crude and ineffective as a selling approach than the one he normally uses. He may be so tense that he forgets vital points of detail in his presentation, and try as the customer may, no clear concept of the product is received. Or he may lose interest and merely go through the motions. The salesman's agitation or despondency colors his attitudes and gives the customer an unfavorable impression of him. All of these consequences lessen the likelihood that a sale will be made during this interview, and even more, during the subsequent ones. Maybe tomorrow will be even worse.

Keep in mind that there are many reasons, outside your control, why prospects may not want to purchase despite your very best selling efforts. Remember that an interview with one customer is something entirely separate from an interview with another. These considerations can aid you to avoid the kind of downward spiral that has been described. It is natural for people to expect that hard work will receive its reward and to feel unsettled when one, two, and then three successive efforts bring no result. Yet factors which are outside your control and which tip the balance against the customer's purchasing can and do sometimes occur in several successive sales interviews, their random nature being mistaken for regularity. This is not to suggest that successive turndowns should always be attributed to bad luck. It is better for you constantly to critique your selling performance and to make any necessary changes that will increase your effectiveness. You do this best by remaining calm and examining what the problem may be. If you detect no problem, it is perfectly logical to attribute the lost sale to "random or undiscovered" causes and to continue with your usual way of selling with emotions held in check. Continue to keep a lookout for what might still be *undiscovered* (not random) factors that are working against the achievement of sales. This is resiliency—the ability to maintain energetic enthusiasm in the face of apparent failure. It's a test of a man's steadiness and steadfastness in pursuing his goals when things are not falling in place as he might intend them to do.

THE BIG PICTURE

So we have come full circle. Now to return to the beginning. One of the ultimate tests of a man is whether or not he can sell an article or service to a customer during their first encounter. There is an even stiffer test. Can he follow up with more sales the second, third, and fourth times around, enjoying the benefits of a strongly established account?

If you now understand yourself and your customer better, the chances are you'll be more successful with him, initially and repeatedly. In human as well as financial terms, you may find your efforts more rewarding. Considering the issues specifically on a business-logic basis, the soundest response would appear to be that of helping individual customers, or the company which is purchasing, to get full satisfaction from what they buy. Real satisfaction comes from a product as it is used, not from any hopes that are raised beforehand or from any kind of comforting assurance later on which compensates in words for what a product does not provide by itself. Real satisfaction, then, is determined—for better or for worse—during the sales interview; the time at which a customer can either come to understand fully what the product is going to do for him, or what it will not. After he has purchased, satisfaction consists in seeing these expectations fulfilled. A salesman is, in effect, the manager of his customer's expectations. By what he says, he can introduce valid or false expectations into the customer's mind. By what he does not say—in explanation and comment or as an inquiry to test the customer's understanding—he can allow misconceptions to continue, and to bring disillusionment after purchase.

The expanded and repeat business which comes directly through a satisfied customer's reorder or by his favorable comments to other potential purchasers is the essence of progress for a salesman and his company. Many salesmen verbally subscribe to this principle but abandon it to take the advantage of a quick and easy sale. Only one style on the Grid keeps it consistently in mind and backs it with action.

There is a final reason for suggesting that 9,9 is a strong and effective basis for salesmanship. This reason is found in human ethics.

The community gives its endorsement to open, candid, straightforward, fact-based, logic-oriented, and problem-solving human relationships. Where these exist or are growing, the society itself is on the upgrade. These are the values that should undergird the conduct of business in a free and open society. To the degree that selling and purchasing are based upon 9,9 mutual understanding and respect, salesmen and their customers are acting in ways consistent with the ethics of society. Each is making a personal contribution to the strengthening of social fabric. In the final analysis, what's good for you is good for the company you represent and good for the customer that you and your company serve.

References

1. Evans, F. B.: "Selling as a Dyadic Relationship: A New Approach," *The American Behavioral Scientist*, vol. 6, pp. 76–79, May, 1963.
2. The technical literature of behavioral science research on which the Grid is based includes about 400 references. The source of these references is Blake, R. R., and J. S. Mouton: *The Managerial Grid*, Houston: Gulf, 1964. They are not repeated here. The literature to be noted in this book is limited to those sources of pertinence in understanding sales situations.
3. A number of different schools of thought described in widely recognized salesmanship textbooks can be analyzed within the framework of the Grid. These approaches are in widespread use as the basis of training and development. Two texts that summarize and comment on these approaches are Stroh, T. F.: *Salesmanship: Personal Communications and Persuasion in Marketing*, Homewood, Ill.: Irwin, 1966, particularly chaps. 11–15; and Thompson, J. W.: *Selling: A Behavioral Science Approach*, New York: McGraw-Hill, 1966, particularly chap. 9. Strong "stimulus-response" selling techniques are characteristic of the 9,1 salesman style. A muted version may be employed under 5,5. Some elements of "want-satisfaction" sales strategies are frequently used by 5,5-oriented salesmen. An even more permissive version of this approach is used in 1,9. "Formula selling" in the *attention-interest-desire-action* sequence and its variants is consistent with 5,5-oriented salesmanship assumptions. "Barrier selling" involves getting the prospect to respond affirmatively to successive points during the sales presentation so that in effect he builds a barrier between himself and the possibility of saying No when the salesman moves to close. It may be used quite forcibly in a 9,1 sales context and in a less directive way under a 5,5 orientation. The "problem solving in a mood of sincerity" or "service concept"

has some outward resemblance to 9,9 but may not be consistent with this Sales Grid style. The reason is that "mood selling" may be used as a technique to obtain the customer's approval and trust, rather than as a basic orientation that is expressed in characteristic behavior throughout the sales interview and in business situations generally. "Depth selling" is a judicious combination of the five previously mentioned techniques and in this way resembles "statistical 5,5," where the salesman relies on the situation for his cues rather than relying on himself to create a positive situation. It also carries overtones of 9,9 but contains some inherent inconsistencies and manipulative characteristics which are discussed in chap. 10 of this book.

4. These characteristics may be wholly or partly sound, and occasionally extremely unsound, verging on deliberate deception. For examples of the latter, see "Flimflam: The 10 Most Deceptive Sales Practices of 1968—So Far," *Sales Management*, vol. 101, pp. 33–36, Sept. 15, 1968.

5. For a discussion of classifications of personal selling, see Stroh: *op. cit.*, pp. 9–10.

6. Blake, R. R., and J. S. Mouton: *The Managerial Grid: An Exploration of Key Managerial Orientations*, Austin, Tex.: Scientific Methods, 1962.

7. Levitt, T.: *Innovation in Marketing: New Perspectives for Profit and Growth*, New York: McGraw-Hill, 1962.

8. The question of What is value? is a long-standing and continuing problem in Economics. What can be said with reasoned assurance is that there is a hierarchy of wants that is unique for each customer at any particular time. There exists no objective basis for ascribing inherent value to any particular product or service. See Georgescu-Roegen, N.: "Utility," *International Encyclopedia of the Social Sciences*, New York: Crowell, Collier, and Macmillan, 1968, vol. 16, pp. 236–267.

9. Cf. Levitt: *op. cit.*, pp. 2–4; Mason, J. L.: "The Low Prestige of Personal Selling," *Journal of Marketing*, vol. 29, pp. 7–10, October, 1965; *Sales Management, loc. cit.*

10. Items taken from *A Grid Self-analysis for Sales Excellence*, Austin, Tex.: Scientific Methods, 1969.

11. Items taken from *ibid*.

12. A 1,9-oriented salesman is likely to find that elements of the "want-satisfaction" approach to selling suit his personal inclinations. The rationale of the "want-satisfaction" method is that a salesman engages in apparently social conversation with the customer at the beginning of the interview so as to get an idea, from what the customer says, of what his strongest interests are. What does he respond to most enthusiastically, what gives him pleasure? As soon as the salesman has diagnosed these "wants," he then concentrates on persuading the customer that the product will give him satisfaction. Want-satisfaction techniques are sometimes employed when selling to purchasing agents, wholesalers, and retail store proprietors, as well as in retail selling. For illustrative descriptions, see Stroh: *op. cit.*, pp. 189–193.

The 1,9-oriented salesman takes the first step—social conversation—in the want-satisfaction selling technique, but does not follow through. The customer's wants are taken as given. The salesman does not actively try to diagnose the customer's underlying desires and then relate his presentation to them. Instead, he believes that once a friendly relationship has been established and the product placed before the customer, a sale will follow as a direct consequence of the mutual good feeling —either now or later.

13. Items taken from *A Grid Self-analysis for Sales Excellence*, Austin, Tex.: Scientific Methods, 1969.

14. Hattwick, M. S.: *The New Psychology of Selling*, New York: McGraw-Hill, 1960, pp. 57–59.

15. This is "want-satisfaction" selling in a 5,5 context. See Note 12, *supra*.

16. Georgescu-Roegen: *op. cit.*, p. 262. See also the description of "bait and switch" techniques in *Sales Management*, *op. cit.*
17. A 5,5 version of "barrier selling." See Note 3, *supra.*
18. A particularly apt description of this dynamic has been provided by Husband, R. W.: *The Psychology of Successful Selling*, New York: Harper, 1953, pp. 193–194.
19. Items taken from *A Grid Self-analysis for Sales Excellence*, Austin, Tex.: Scientific Methods, 1969.
20. For a detailed explanation of the marketing concept and its implications, see Levitt: *op. cit.* Ways of diagnosing a company's current approach to its market, redefining the market in terms of an ideal strategic model, and implementing organization development in the direction of heightened corporate goals are discussed in Blake, R. R., and J. S. Mouton: *Corporate Excellence Through Grid Organization Development*, Houston: Gulf, 1968, pp. 216–219; and *Corporate Excellence Diagnosis*, Austin, Tex.: Scientific Methods, 1968, pp. 201–266.
21. For discussion of the continuing development of a company's product line and the elimination of weak products, see Hooper, D. C.: "Planning the Product Line," in H. B. Maynard (ed.), *Handbook of Business Administration*, New York: McGraw-Hill, 1967, pp. 8–24 to 8–36.
22. Items taken from *A Grid Self-analysis for Sales Excellence*, Austin, Tex.: Scientific Methods, 1969.
23. Niland, P.: *Management Problems in the Acquisition of Special Automatic Equipment*, Boston: Harvard Graduate School of Business Administration, 1961.
24. "Nobody Here Knows Who Carborundum Is," *Sales Management*, vol. 101, pp. 31–33, July 1, 1968.
25. Farmer, S. C.: "Dynamic Purchasing," in Maynard (ed.), *op. cit.*, pp. 6–35 to 6–43.
26. Rieser, C.: "The Salesman Isn't Dead—He's Different," *Fortune*, vol. 66, pp. 124–127, 248, 252, 254, 259, November, 1962.
27. The general character of 9,9 team management and team action is described in Blake, R. R., and J. S. Mouton: *The Managerial Grid*, Houston: Gulf, 1964, chap. 7; and *Corporate Excellence Through Grid Organization Development*, Houston: Gulf, 1968, chap. 5. Types and styles of interaction between groups are considered in Blake, R. R., H. A. Shepard, and J. S. Mouton: *Managing Intergroup Conflict in Industry*, Houston: Gulf, 1964. See also Blake and Mouton (1968): *op. cit.*, chaps. 7 and 8.
28. There are other approaches which are not deceitful in the facade sense, but which are not "pure" in the manner of the styles depicted in chaps. 4 to 8. These include circumstances where two or more sets of assumptions are successively or simultaneously employed by a salesman. Paternalistic selling, for example, is based on 9,1 concern for pushing the product and 1,9 concern for being liked. Other approaches include counterbalancing; the 9,1–1,1 win-or-leave cycle; the 9,1–1,9 wide-arc pendulum swing; and statistical 5,5. Because these are not sufficiently common in everyday selling situations, they are not elaborated here. See Blake, R. R., and J. S. Mouton: *The Managerial Grid*, Houston: Gulf, 1964, chap. 9.
29. A classic example of this is Iago's deception of Othello and others in Shakespeare's play.
30. The recognition and use of positive features of a good reputation are not always stimulated by facade tactics. See Husband: *op. cit.*, p. 71.
31. Carnegie, D.: *How to Win Friends and Influence People*, New York: Pocket Books, 1958, p. 28.
32. Nirenberg, J. S.: *Getting Through to People*, Englewood Cliffs, N.J.: Prentice-Hall, 1969.

33. Blake, R. R., and J. S. Mouton: *Corporate Excellence Through Grid Organization Development,* Houston: Gulf, 1968, pp. 54–56.
34. Korzybski, A.: "The Role of Language in the Perceptual Processes," in R. R. Blake and G. V. Ramsey (eds.), *Perception: An Approach to Personality,* New York: Ronald, 1951, pp. 170–205.
35. Webster, F. E., Jr.: "Interpersonal Communication and Salesman Effectiveness," *Journal of Marketing,* vol. 32, pp. 7–13, July, 1968.
36. A third dimension has been added to the Grid. However, it complicates the analysis of situations without adding appreciably to insights into the situations themselves. Thus, no use is made of it in this book. See Blake, R. R., and J. S. Mouton: "The Managerial Grid in Three Dimensions," *Training and Development Journal,* vol. 21, no. 1, pp. 2–5, January, 1967.

Index

Index

Numerals indicating Grid styles are in italic type.